Andrew Carnegie

앤드류 카네기

Biography Comic
who? ❷❹ Andrew Carnegie

초판 1쇄 인쇄 2011년 4월 8일
초판 2쇄 발행 2013년 7월 5일

지은이 오영석
그린이 스튜디오 청비
번역 채드 워커
감수 김수희
펴낸이 김선식

Chief Story Creator 김정미
Story Creator 채정은
Design Creator 김경민
Marketing Creator 신문수

4th Creative Story Team 김선영, 이유미, 김선민, 전해인, 최수아
Creative Design Dept. 박효영
Creative Management Team 김성자, 송현주, 권송이, 김민아, 윤이경, 한선미
Creative Marketing Dept. 최창규, 이주화, 이상혁, 박현미, 백미숙
Communication Team 서선행
Contents Rights Team 김미영

펴낸곳 (주)다산북스
주소 서울시 마포구 서교동 395-27번지
전화 02-702-1724(기획편집) 02-703-1725(마케팅) 02-704-1724(경영지원)
팩스 02-703-2219
이메일 dasanbooks@hanmail.net
홈페이지 www.dasanbooks.com
출판등록 2005년 12월 23일 제313-2005-00277호

필름 출력 스크린그래픽센타 **종이** 월드페이퍼(주) **인쇄·제본** (주)현문

ISBN 978-89-6370-452-4 14740
SET 978-89-6370-438-8

who?

Andrew Carnegie

앤드류 카네기

글 **오영석** | 그림 **스튜디오 청비** | 번역 **채드 워커** | 감수 **김수희**

Dasan Kid

Andrew Carnegie

American entrepreneur, November 25, 1835 ~ August 11, 1919

Andrew Carnegie, an entrepreneur who led the steel industry, was born in 1835 in a small village in Scotland called Dunfermline. This village and its surrounding area had a developed cotton spinning industry. His father was one of the skillful weavers there, but he ended up losing his job due to the Industrial Revolution. Eventually, the Carnegie family immigrated to the United States to find better opportunity.

Andrew began working at a textiles factory at the age of thirteen. Then several years later, he began working as a telegraph messenger, but when his boss saw that he had the ability to record telegraph messages just by listening to them coming in, he was promoted to telegraph operator.

Later, Andrew began working for the Pennsylvania Railroad Company and at the young age of 24, became the superintendent of the Pittsburgh division. In 1861, the Civil War broke out and Carnegie took part in the war as a telegraph operator. It was there that he saw how important the railroad was for transporting people and goods, and at the age of 28, he created a steel company called Keystone Bridge. Just as Carnegie had predicted, steel soon dominated industries, and his company which produced high-quality steel became very successful.

But then one day, the workers at one of his steel mills went on strike because they were unhappy with the way they were being treated. As a result of this incident, Carnegie thought hard about how he could help in establishing a society in which everyone lived well, regardless of their wealth.

Later, Carnegie established a charity foundation named after himself and built libraries, theaters, and schools in various places around the world. He also created a laborers' fund to help provide for workers after their retirement.

As a top businessman who improved the steel industry around the world, and a great philanthropist who generously gave his own money, Andrew Carnegie continues to be a role model to many people.

앤드류 카네기

미국의 기업인, 1835년 11월 25일 ~ 1919년 8월 11일

미국의 철강 산업을 이끈 사업가 앤드류 카네기는 1835년 스코틀랜드의 시골 마을 던펌린에서 태어났습니다. 그가 태어난 던펌린은 방적 산업이 발달한 지역이었습니다. 아버지 역시 그곳에서 활동하는 솜씨 있는 직조공 중 한 명이었지만 산업 혁명의 물결이 일면서 일거리를 잃게 되었습니다. 결국 카네기 가족은 일자리를 찾아 미국으로 이민을 갑니다.

카네기는 13살부터 방적 공장에서 일하기 시작했습니다. 그리고 몇 년 후에는 전보 배달원 일을 시작하였는데, 소리만으로 전보의 내용을 기록하는 능력을 인정받아 전신 기사로 임명됩니다.

이후 카네기는 펜실베니아 철도 회사로 자리를 옮겨 24세의 젊은 나이에 피츠버그 지역의 책임자가 되면서 주목을 받았습니다. 1861년, 남북 전쟁이 발발하자 카네기는 전신 기사로 전쟁에 참여합니다. 그곳에서 사람과 물자를 운송하는 철도의 중요성을 절감한 그는 28세에 키스톤 브리지라는 철 회사를 설립했습니다. 머지않아 그의 생각대로 철이 산업을 지배하는 시대가 왔고, 품질 높은 강철을 생산하던 카네기의 회사는 큰 성공을 거두게 됩니다.

그러던 어느 날, 카네기가 운영하는 제강소에서 노동자들의 파업이 일어납니다. 자신들의 처우에 대한 불만이 그 원인이었습니다. 카네기는 이 사건을 계기로 돈이 많고 적음에 상관없이 모두 잘 살 수 있는 사회를 만들기 위한 방법을 고민하게 됩니다.

이후 카네기는 자신의 이름을 내건 자선 재단을 세워 세계 곳곳에 도서관과 공연장을 짓고, 학교를 세웠으며, 노동자들을 위한 기금을 만들어 은퇴 후에도 안정된 삶을 살 수 있게 도왔습니다.

카네기는 전 세계 철강 산업을 발전시킨 최고의 경영자로, 자신의 재산을 아낌없이 내 놓은 위대한 기부가로 오늘날까지 많은 사람들의 귀감이 되고 있습니다.

이 책을 만든 사람들

글 · 오영석

어린이들이 재미있고 신나게 읽을 수 있는 책을 쓰기 위해 노력하는 작가입니다. 나와 똑같이 고민하고, 실패했던 위인들의 이야기를 통해 독자들도 '할 수 있다'는 마음을 가지길 바랍니다. 작품으로 『세계사 한국사』, 『과학 교과 주제 탐구Q. 몸』, 『걸어서 세계 속으로 2. 일본』 등이 있습니다.

그림 · 스튜디오 청비

어린이들을 위해 새롭고, 재미있고, 즐거운 이야깃거리를 만드는 만화 창작 집단입니다. 세상을 바꾼 인물들의 삶을 통해 어린이들이 희망찬 미래를 만들어가길 바랍니다. 작품으로 『지식 똑똑 경제 리더십 탐구-긍정의 힘』, 『why? 서양 근대 사회의 시작』, 『why? 세계대전과 전후의 세계』 등이 있습니다. 이 책은 이준형 작가님이 그림을 그리셨습니다.

번역 · 채드 워커(Chad Walker)

미국 텍사스 오스틴에서 심리학과 일본어를 전공했습니다. 일본으로 건너가 10년 간 살았고 이후 한국과 중국을 오가며 한 · 중 · 일의 동아시아 문화를 비교 연구하고 있습니다. 현재는 연세대학교 국어국문학과 박사 과정 중에 있습니다. 옮긴 책으로 『한국어 교육을 위한 한국어 연어사전』, 『한국인의 가치 문화』, 『속성 한국어』 등이 있습니다.

감수 · 김수희

연세대학교에서 역사를 전공했습니다. 이후 한국뿐 아니라 일본, 미국에서 한국어, 일본어, 영어를 가르쳐 왔으며 부모를 위한 영어교육용 책을 썼습니다. 영어교육채널 EBSe '엄마표 영어특강'에서 강의를 하며 홈스쿨, 알파벳과 파닉스, 다차원 테마 영어 수업 기법을 알리고 있습니다. 전국 각지에서 어린이 영어 교육에 대한 강연을 하며 창의적이고 열정적인 교수법으로 영어를 배우고자 하는 어린이와 부모들에게 많은 도움을 주고 있습니다.

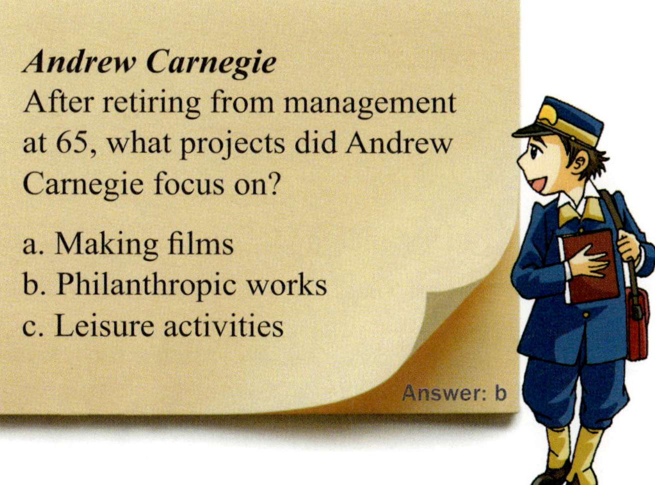

Contents

01 The Son of a Weaver

D-d-don't push me!
Umph!
Heh-heh, consider that the price for being first, Andrew.
Hungry, Bill? I may have lost the race, but I grabbed the most grass.

Thomas, eat lots and lots to grow up real strong!
Hey, my Henry's the tallest!
My, just look at them play.

CLICK
CLACK
CLICK
CLACK
I'm home!
Just in time for dinner.
Haha, I see.
I tried to come earlier, but the rabbits were just so much fun...
You all are free to eat as well.
Yes, Mr. Carnegie.
Wow, it looks delicious!

Andrew, has your rabbit grown any?
Yes!
I see your friends like those rabbits more than you!
Well, each rabbit is named after each of my friends who help feed them. Everyone really got into it.
So how did you come up with that idea?
Well, there's too many babies to feed by myself but doing it together with my friends saves time, and all the rabbits get enough food, too.
Well, you certainly know how to work efficiently. You'll be ready to take over the business someday.
But dear, isn't there less and less work coming in these days?
Yes, and it's due to all the factory-produced cheap fabrics out there. But don't worry, the materials we weave are of much greater quality.

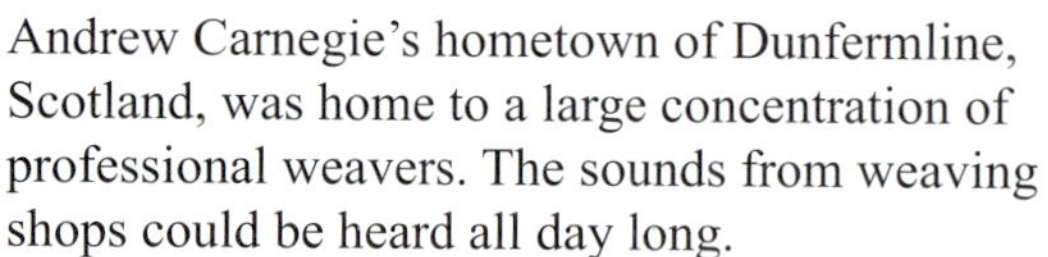

Andrew Carnegie's hometown of Dunfermline, Scotland, was home to a large concentration of professional weavers. The sounds from weaving shops could be heard all day long.

Andrew's father, William Carnegie, was a skilled weaver himself. However, the Industrial Revolution* brought in numerous textile mills, which meant there were fewer jobs for weavers. Textile mills could produce and sell materials in large quantities at a much lower price than those made by hand by weavers.

Buyers preferred the cheaper and more readily available materials made at the mills, despite the fact that materials made by skilled weavers were of better quality.

*Industrial Revolution: A great social change that occurred in the latter half of the 18th century characterized by the beginning of large-scale, mass production of goods in factories.

Eventually William had to lay off his assistants and start getting rid of his looms.
Be careful with that.
Thank you.
I've loaded them all except for one, just as you requested. Here's your money.
Heave-ho!
Mr. Carnegie, nobody wants to buy looms these days. Therefore I can't offer you much. If you've changed your mind I'll return them to you.
Oh my.
Is this all? This isn't even half of what I paid for them.

Oh dear.
Oh, what's this?
I sold some of the looms. We can get by on this for a while.
Oh no! Will we be okay, dear?
There's no other alternative. I'm going to find a job, so just be patient.

Despite his family's financial situation getting worse and worse, Andrew continued to grow up happy and healthy because he was still too young to understand.
I'm home from school!
?
Ah, back from school, I see?
Dad, that's odd. Where did the looms go?
Um, I packed them up so we can move into an even better place.
Where? Are we moving to a bigger house?
Well, it's not a bad house.
Woo-hoo! Yippee!
17

Soon the Carnegies moved to their new home.
However, the new house was not anything like they had imagined. Andrew was very disappointed when he saw the shabby old house.
Andrew, starting today I'm going to sell vegetables. Would you like to help me?
It's hard for your father to be the only one working. So I'm going to help out.
But why do you have to all of a sudden?

Although his parents were always cheerful and in good spirits, Andrew knew what had happened. His family had become poor.

Seeing that things weren't getting better for them even after the move, Andrew's parents discussed emigrating to the United States.

They say America is the land of opportunity.

But this is all happening too fast. Besides, even if we combined all our savings we can't afford the boat fare.

If we go, I'm sure there will be lots of work and so we can earn more money.

Well, that certainly would be nice...

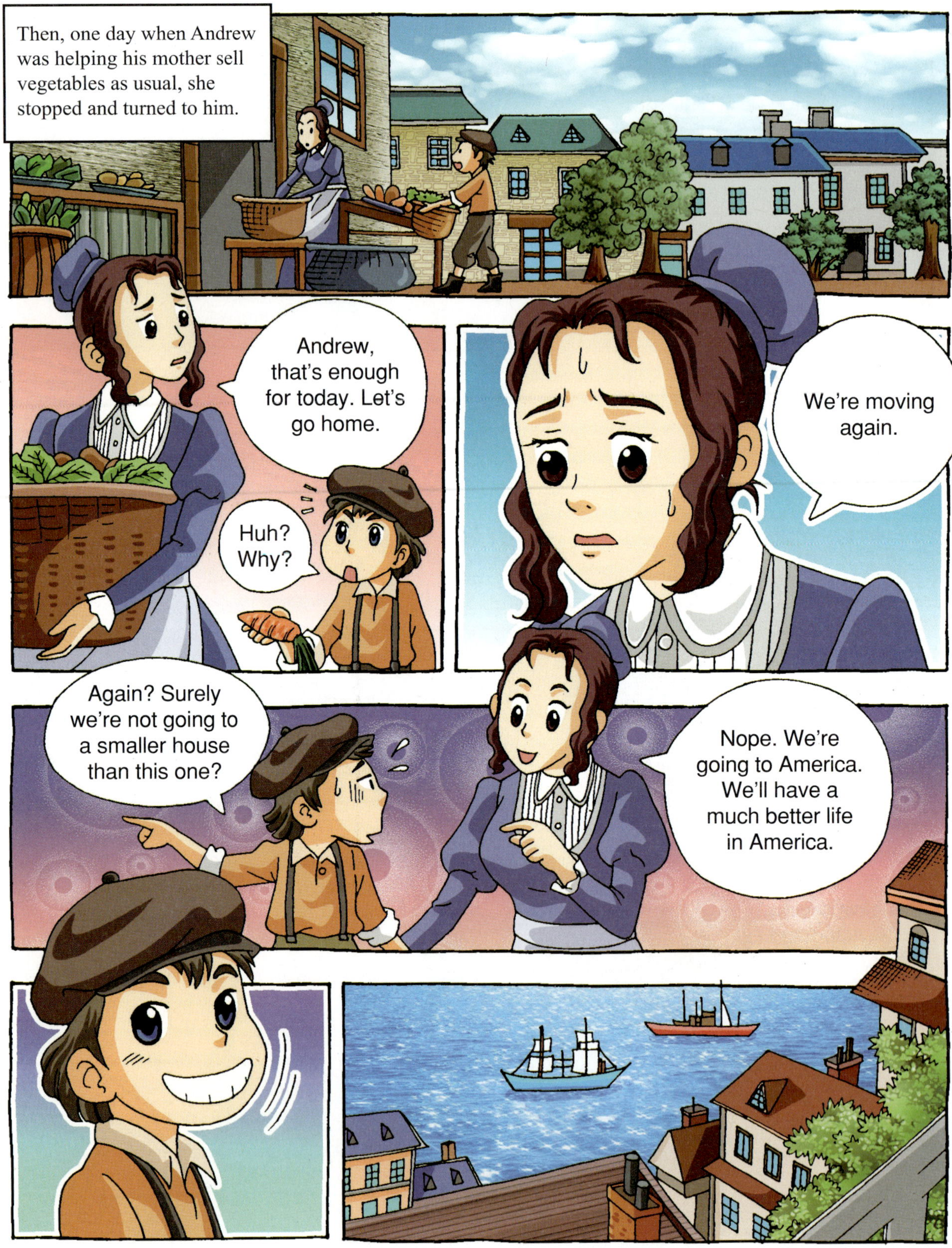

Then, one day when Andrew was helping his mother sell vegetables as usual, she stopped and turned to him.

Andrew, that's enough for today. Let's go home.

Huh? Why?

We're moving again.

Again? Surely we're not going to a smaller house than this one?

Nope. We're going to America. We'll have a much better life in America.

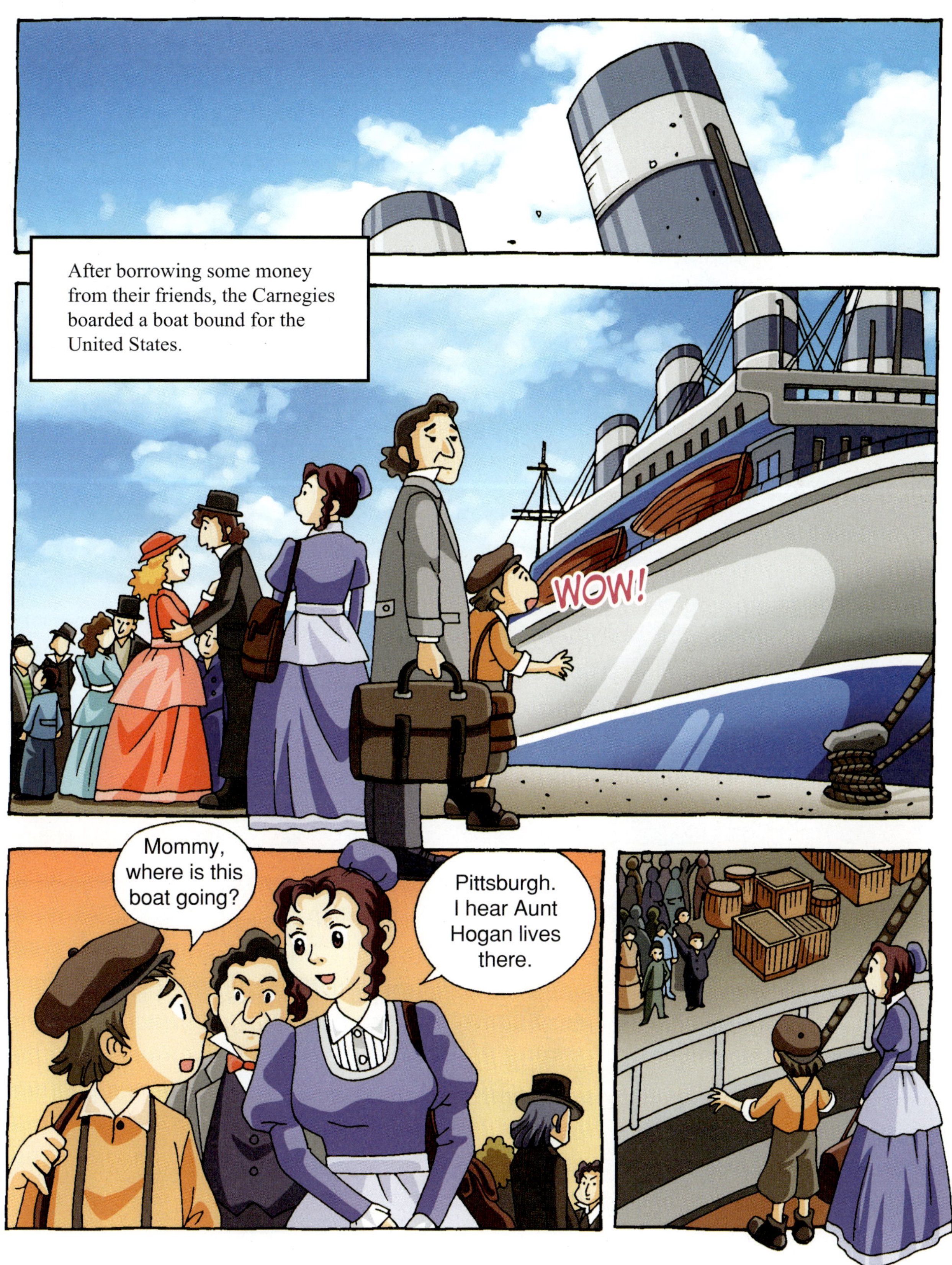

After borrowing some money from their friends, the Carnegies boarded a boat bound for the United States.
WOW!
Mommy, where is this boat going?
Pittsburgh. I hear Aunt Hogan lives there.

Pittsburgh?
Andrew, once we get there I'm going to start weaving again. I'll buy us good things to eat, and send you to a good school.
Really?
TOOT
Farewell!
TOOOT!
Godspeed!

The Carnegies talked about their new life in America, and their hearts filled with hope.
Everything's going to be alright from now on, right?
Of course! In America, the things I weave will sell like hotcakes!
Huh?
Farewell Scotland! I'll be back someday!

02

Off to Work

In 1848, the Carnegie family arrived in Pittsburgh, USA, where they were greeted by the Hogans, the family who had invited them to come live there.

The Carnegies were to live in a suburban working class housing area. The streets were lined with shabby wooden houses.

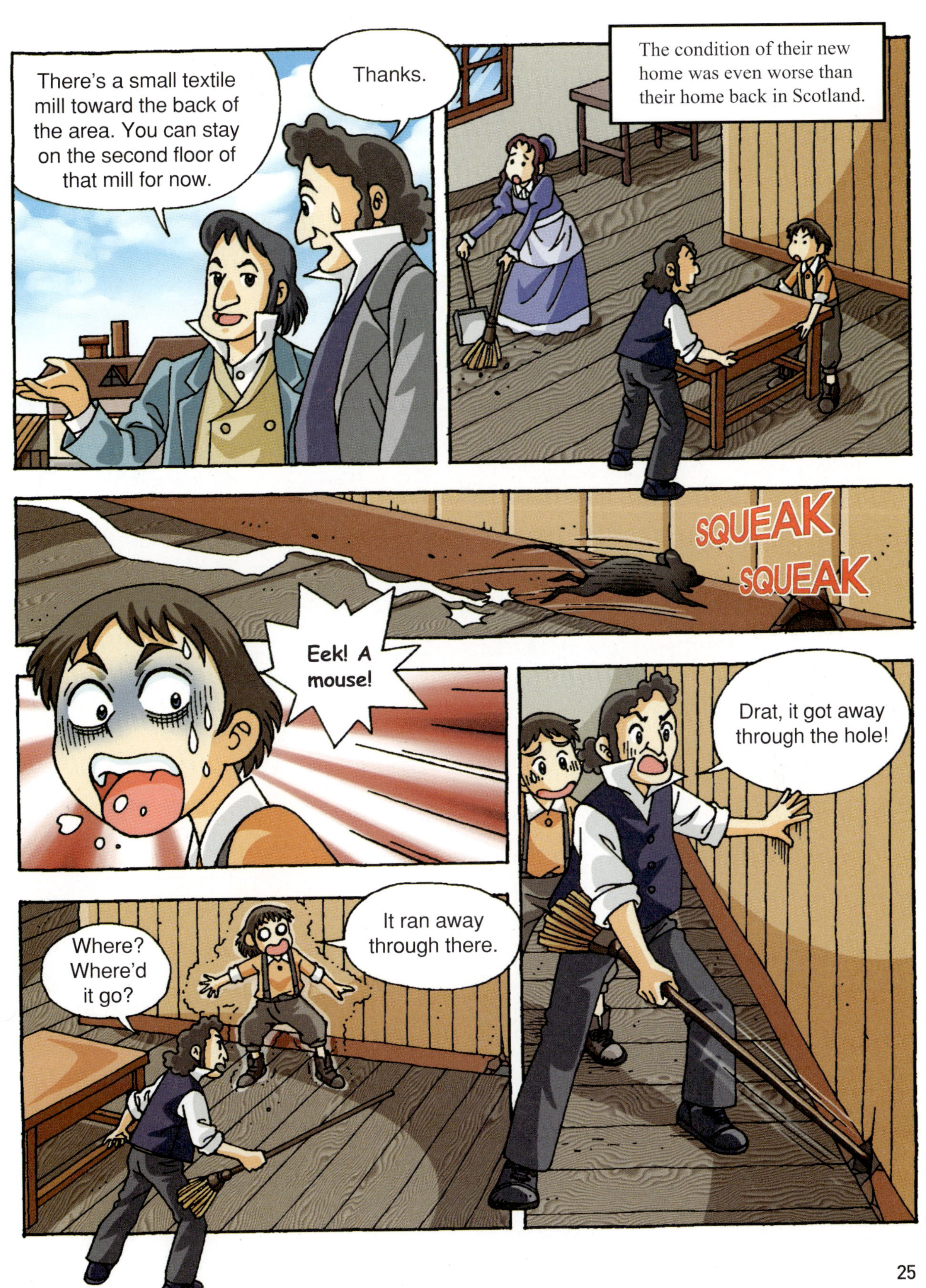
There's a small textile mill toward the back of the area. You can stay on the second floor of that mill for now.
Thanks.
The condition of their new home was even worse than their home back in Scotland.
SQUEAK
SQUEAK
Eek! A mouse!
Drat, it got away through the hole!
Where? Where'd it go?
It ran away through there.

Dear, do you think we made the right choice coming here?
But William's textiles did not sell well because cheap factory textiles were already becoming popular in America.
Don't worry. Once my skill becomes known, the orders will pour in. Then we can move to a better place.
Andrew's mother Margaret once again rolled up her sleeves and started working.
Heave-ho!
I got a job at the shoe binder's. Your mom's gonna work, too.
What are you doing?
Can I help you?
No, Andrew. You should be studying.

Ow!
THWACK
Are you okay?
I-I'm fine. Don't worry.
Oh, if only I could earn some money to help us...
Andrew, come with me!
Okay, be right there!

You're aware that we're not doing as well as we used to, right?
Yes, Father.
Now that you're thirteen, I think you should start working. I'm sorry if it takes away from your time for schoolwork.
No, no. I was actually hoping I could start working to help out our family.
I hear there are some jobs available at the Blackstone cotton mill. Let's go check it out together.
Great! If they'll just give me a chance I'll do my very best.

William and Andrew started working at the cotton mill from 6:00 a.m. to 6:00 p.m. The mill was far from home, so they had to walk a long distance every day.
That's my boy.
It's so nice that we get to work together.
I'm so sorry, Andrew. You're so smart, and yet you have to work like this.
WHIRRR
At the cotton mill, Andrew worked as a bobbin boy. Bobbins were the spools of thread used at the mill, and the job of a bobbin boy was to change out used spools of thread with new ones.

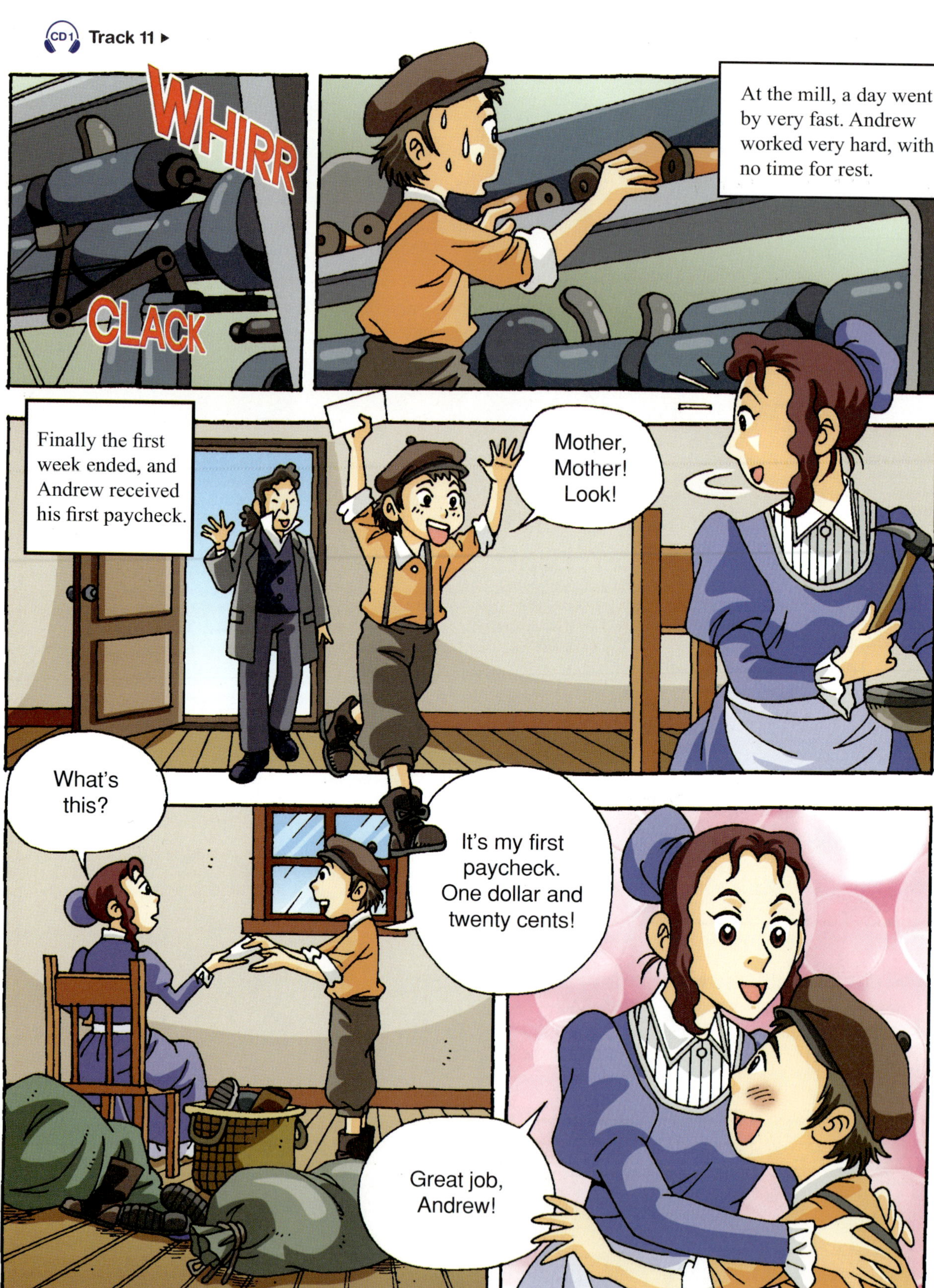

WHIRR
CLACK
At the mill, a day went by very fast. Andrew worked very hard, with no time for rest.
Finally the first week ended, and Andrew received his first paycheck.
Mother, Mother! Look!
What's this?
It's my first paycheck. One dollar and twenty cents!
Great job, Andrew!

But Andrew's excitement didn't last long. The job of bobbin boy for a factory that never stopped producing was just too much for a young boy of thirteen.
WHIRRR
WHIRR
I feel... dizzy.
Andrew!
Yes, foreman!
Go to the boiler room and check the temperature.
Yes, sir.
Andrew, put those bobbins in the oil tank!
Okay, I'll do it after I go to the boiler room.

Then, one evening the Carnegies were visited by a guest with good news.

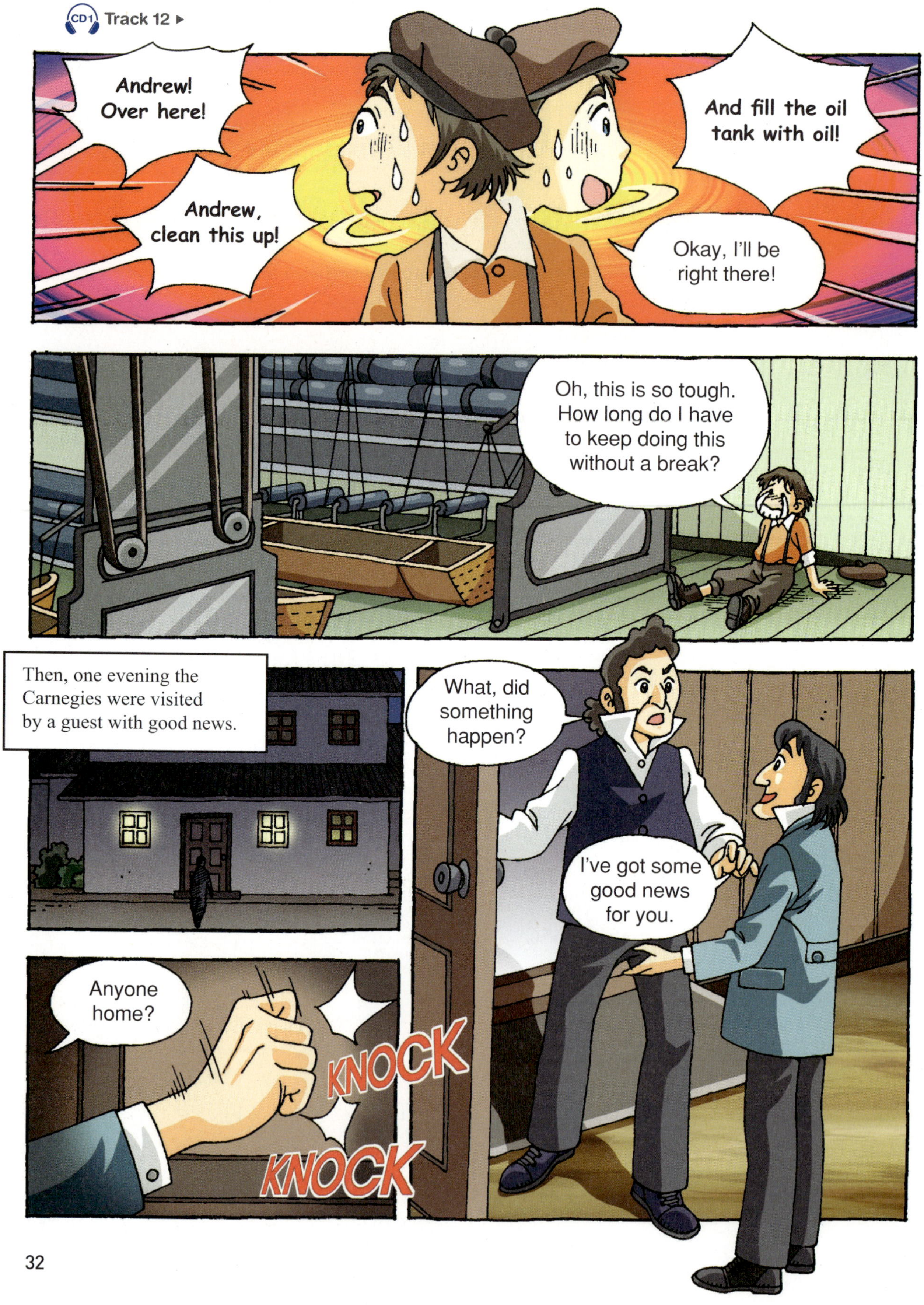

The telegraph office is hiring a telegraph messenger boy, and I thought Andrew might be good for the job. It pays a lot better than what they offer at the cotton mill.
Telegraph messenger? But Andrew still doesn't even know the names of the streets in Pittsburgh.
I'll do it. I wanna do it!
Andrew?
Father, I can do the job well. Please let me do it.

*Morse code: A code system for transmitting telegraphs in which the letters of the alphabet and numbers are represented by sequences of dots and dashes.

Andrew soon memorized all of the street addresses in Pittsburgh, and before long he had become the fastest messenger boy in the city.

You may come in and leave it here.
CREAK
WOW

What's the matter?
I've never seen so many books.
Looks like you like books.
Um, yes.
Really? I'm sure you've read a few.
Not that many, actually. We have no money to buy books...
You can borrow any books if you want to read. Actually, I lend out my books every Saturday.
So... I too can borrow some books?
Of course. Just bring them back next Saturday after you read them.
Thank you, Mr. Anderson!

Andrew met a lot of good people while delivering telegrams. Meeting them allowed Andrew to learn things he hadn't had the opportunity to learn before.
Then, one day Andrew experienced something new.
Is the operator still not back?
That appears to be the case. Please wait a bit longer.

Whew, so many telegraphs have arrived. Where did the operator go?
CLICK
CLICK
CLICK
CLICK
CLICK
Curious about the content of the telegrams, Andrew listened carefully to the sounds of the telegraph machine as it punched out the Morse code. Then he compared what he heard to the decoded output of the machine.
CLICK
Then, a few days later, the operator was absent once again.
The operator's gone again?
?

CLICK CLACK
...will arrive tomorrow...
Oh my, I'm so sorry. I'll decode it as soon as possible.
That's okay. I've already decoded it. I'll deliver it now.
What? How did you learn the code?
I learnt to recognise these sound patterns coming from the machine.
Really? Well, let's see.

Uh?
Hm?
Impossible!
There's not even one wrong letter!
Andrew! You're really something. I only know of two people who can decode directly from the sounds.
Really?
Amazing!

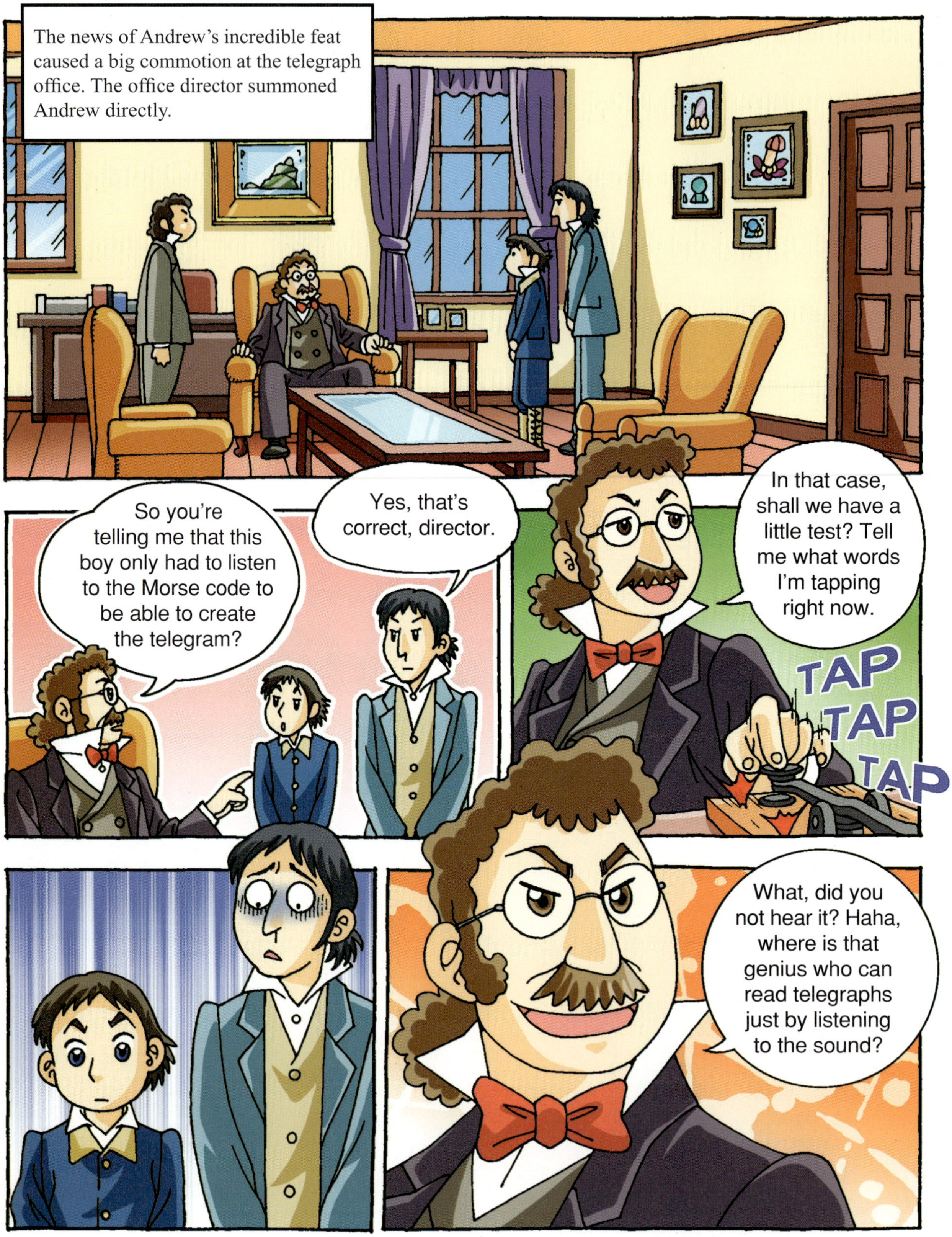

The news of Andrew's incredible feat caused a big commotion at the telegraph office. The office director summoned Andrew directly.

Oh, I'm sorry. I wasn't sure if you were done yet. You tapped "Pittsburgh Bound Train, 1:00."
Wh-what's your name, boy?
Andrew Carnegie,
Yes, sir.
Carnegie. It's time for you to quit being a messenger. Starting today I'm promoting you to telegraph operator.

Mother!
What's the matter?
I'm, I'm... telegraph... telegraph operator!
A telegraph operator did what?
I said I've become a telegraph operator!
What?

By being able to decipher telegrams by listening only to the sounds of the telegraph machine, Andrew was able to work much faster than the other telegraph operators. Thanks to Andrew, his family was now able to repay the debt they incurred when leaving Scotland. Andrew had been working at the telegraph office for only one and a half years.

03

Working for the Railroad

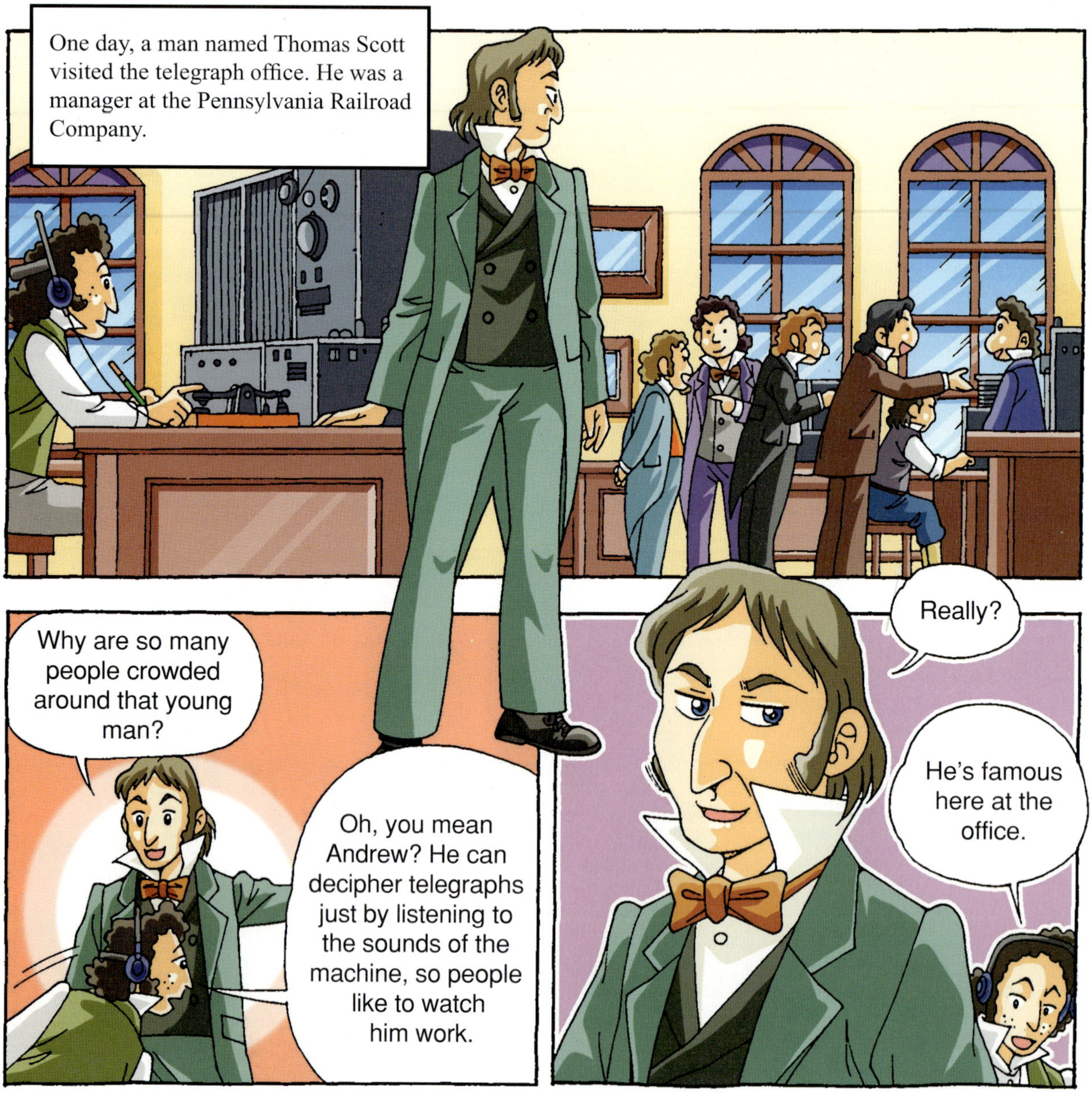

TAP
TAP
TAP TAP
TAP
Woo-hoo!
Simply amazing, no matter how you look at it!
He's still so young, and so talented. I bet he's got a lot of ambition.

After witnessing Andrew's talent, Scott soon became a regular visitor to the telegraph office.
Andrew, can we talk for a minute?
Oh, Mr. Scott. Would you like to send a telegram?
Today I didn't come here to send a telegram. I've got something important to talk to you about.
Talk? To me?
Yes. I was wondering if you would want to come work for us. We can pay you a lot more money.
But Mr. Scott, you work for the Pennsylvania Railroad Company...
It's in the Pittsburgh area.

But I don't know anything about the railroad.
Haha, I'm not asking you to operate a train.
Oh! A train!
Railroad companies need telegraph operators, too. With only one train track for trains going in both directions, we have to use telegraphs to control them to prevent accidents.
AHHHH
What? What's it doing here unannounced?
In that case, I think I'd like to try.
You should have no problems controlling the train operations with your ability. Train collisions are increasing these days.

Andrew was given a job at the Pennsylvania Railroad Company controlling the distance between trains as they moved.

TAP TA TAP

The westbound train will wait at the station while the eastbound train passes through.

SLAM

HUH

Mr. Scott!

What's happened?
Andrew, there's been an accident!
What? Did two trains collide?
No, there's no problem with our freight trains. A passenger train had an accident, and as a result all of our trains have had to stop.
The tracks must be in chaos! We've got to get this fixed quick.
That's why we need Mr. Scott here right away...
What should we do? He still hasn't come in to work.
Oh, this is bad. Without Mr. Scott here, who's going to fix this?
What?
Oh no.

What should we do? If the trains remain stopped, their cargo won't arrive on time. And that will cause the company to lose a lot of money.

What are we gonna do?

We can't just wait around for something to happen. I'll telegraph our trains to tell them to move.

What? Andrew, you can't make such decisions on your own. You have no orders from a superior!
Saving the trust people have in our company is more important than that. We have no other choice!

But... if you make a mistake, you'll be fired.

Fired?

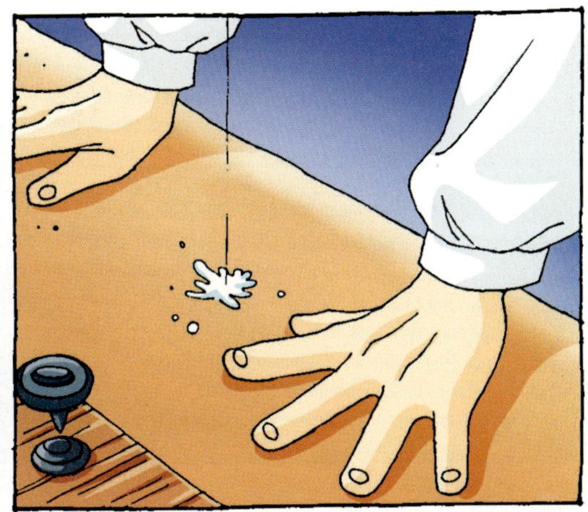

TAP

But we've really got no other option.

TAP
TAP

Freight train #1 move ahead, train #2 wait. And train #3, proceed slowly.
TAP
TAP

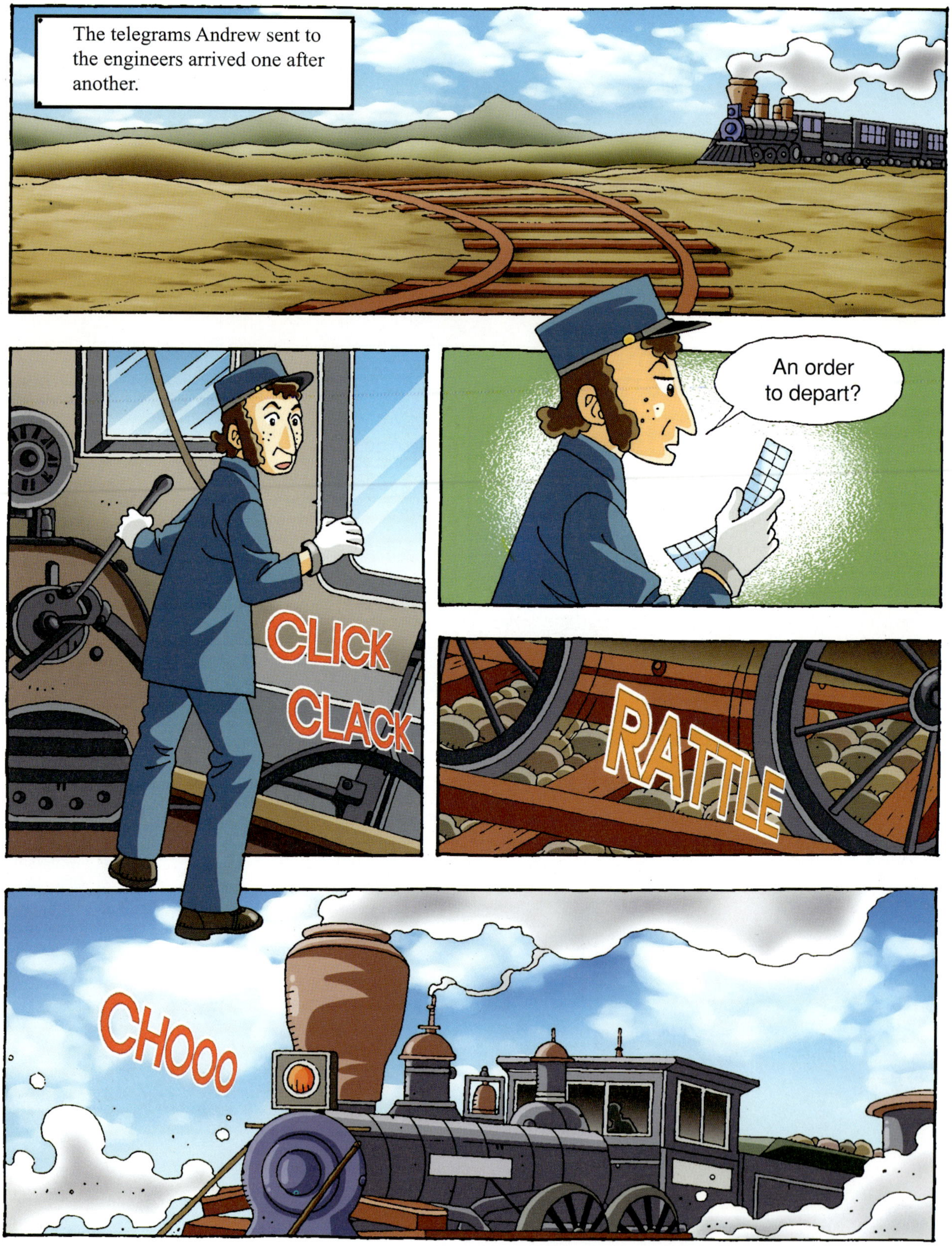

The telegrams Andrew sent to the engineers arrived one after another.
CLICK CLACK
An order to depart?
RATTLE
CHOOO

Prepared to lose his job if he failed, Andrew contacted the trains to get the tracks back in order.

The situation had almost ended.
Andrew, did you hear about the accident?
Oh, Mr. Scott.
Oh my, this will get our freight trains in a big mess. Where do I start...
Um... Mr. Scott, I have something to tell you. Actually I have already telegraphed our trains to get them back on schedule.
What? So, where is our eastbound train right now?
Here are the times and locations for all our trains.

I'm sorry. I deserve to be penalized for deciding to take these actions on my own.

Andrew.
Yes?

You did an amazing job getting the trains back on schedule! Without your help, the trains would have arrived late, and the company would have suffered serious losses.

Does this mean you're forgiving me?
Forgive? I've got a mind to give you even more work to do. Haha!

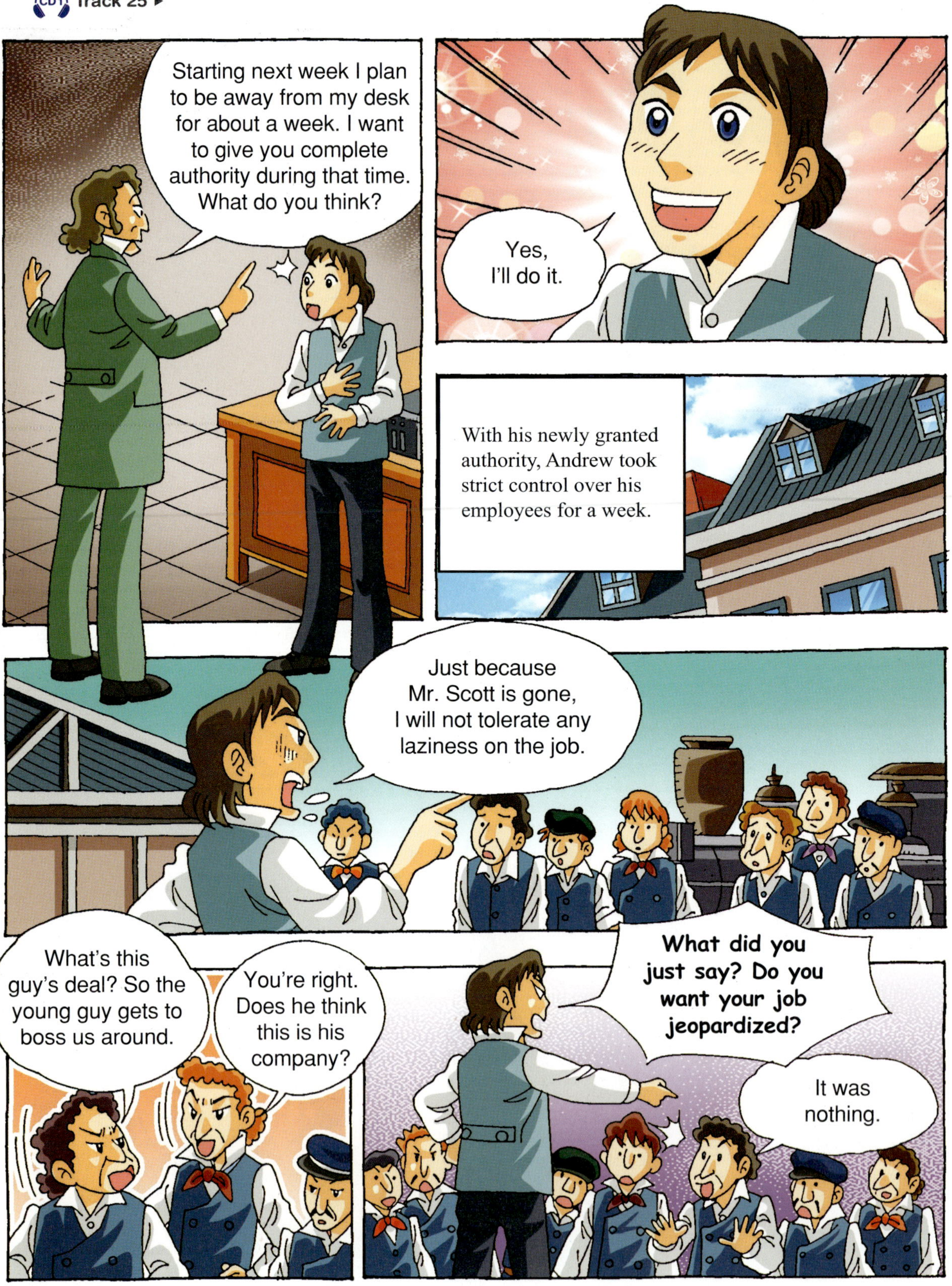

Starting next week I plan to be away from my desk for about a week. I want to give you complete authority during that time. What do you think?

Yes, I'll do it.

With his newly granted authority, Andrew took strict control over his employees for a week.

Just because Mr. Scott is gone, I will not tolerate any laziness on the job.

What's this guy's deal? So the young guy gets to boss us around.

You're right. Does he think this is his company?

What did you just say? Do you want your job jeopardized?

It was nothing.

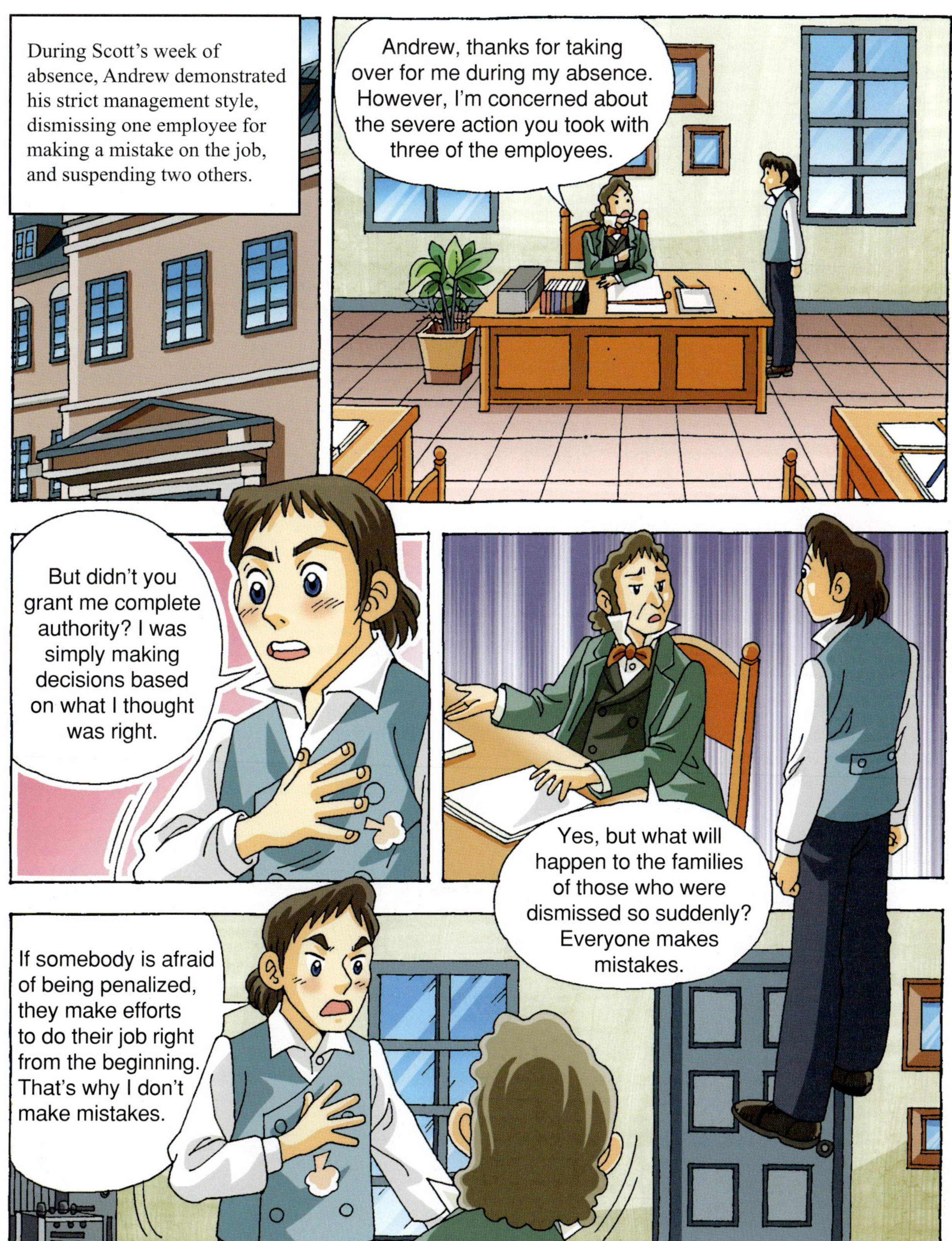

During Scott's week of absence, Andrew demonstrated his strict management style, dismissing one employee for making a mistake on the job, and suspending two others.

Andrew, thanks for taking over for me during my absence. However, I'm concerned about the severe action you took with three of the employees.

But didn't you grant me complete authority? I was simply making decisions based on what I thought was right.

Yes, but what will happen to the families of those who were dismissed so suddenly? Everyone makes mistakes.

If somebody is afraid of being penalized, they make efforts to do their job right from the beginning. That's why I don't make mistakes.

The next morning, Andrew was on his way back to Pittsburgh after picking up the employee salary checks from the company's main office.

Where are they?
What's the matter?
Oh no!
Back the train up! Back up! Please!

SCREEEH
CHOO CHOO
The bundle of paychecks had flown off the train while Andrew was enjoying a conversation with the train engineer. The train slowly backed up, and Andrew was able to find the checks along the riverbank.
There it is!
WOOOSH
I'm so lucky.

Everyone makes mistakes.
I don't make mistakes.
At that moment Andrew realized his big mistake. From that day forward, he changed his attitude toward employees.
Now I know just how harsh I was on those employees.
Years later, Scott became vice-president of the Pennsylvania Railroad Company and returned to the main office. Andrew took over his position as superintendent of the Pittsburgh division. As the new superintendent, Andrew took good care of his employees.
Don't you think Andrew has changed?
Yeah. Even if we make a mistake, he smiles and tells us it's okay.
Yes...
It's alright. Good job~

What are you guys talking about?
Eek!
Oh, it's nothing, Mr. Carnegie.

Why don't you take a short break? It's not good to work nonstop all day long.

What was that?
Haha, I think I'm going to like Mr. Carnegie.

Andrew's changed attitude had a positive effect on his employees. Even those who ignored him because he was so young, and even those who disliked him because he had been so strict gradually began to warm to him as their employer. Soon the Pittsburgh office was turning big profits.

Still only 24 years old, Andrew, with total confidence in accomplishing whatever he set out to do, had become a district superintendent. With an understanding heart toward whomever he was dealing with, he was very successful in his new position.

District Superintendent
Andrew Carnegie

04

The Civil War

*emancipation of slaves: The abolition of slavery and the provision of rights and opportunities to slaves as free men and women.

Andrew, I've been given the task of transporting armaments from Washington for the war. We need some assistance, so would you be able to come and help?
Andrew hurried to Washington after receiving Scott's telegram.
Mr. Scott, I made it.
Andrew, so good to see you.
TAP TAP

How have you been?
Let's dispense with the formalities, Andrew. Here, look at this.
The South has severed all telegraph lines, and the Union armies can't communicate with each other. And during all the confusion, apparently the South have blocked the railroad tracks as well.
Oh no, we're in trouble.
Right. At this rate we won't be able to supply the Union with the supplies it needs. The soldiers will be exhausted before they even reach the battlefield.
What can I do to help?
I want you to first try to reconnect the severed railroad tracks. You've got to do this as fast as possible. I know it'll be tough, but you need to do it within a week.

A week!

CLANK
THUNK
Oh, this is heavy.
If we could only take a break.
Hold on, everyone!

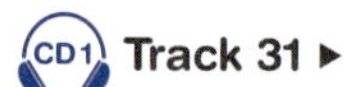

Keep it up! If we're going to win this war, we've got to rebuild the railroad.
I believe we can give the Union army victory.

The rebuilding of the railroads continued nonstop, day and night.

Don't give up. Just think of how important what we're doing is.

Mr. Carnegie, don't you ever get exhausted?
Of course I do. But I'm confident we can change the course of this war, so there's no way I can rest.
R-really? Is the work we're doing really that important?
You bet it is. It wouldn't be an exaggeration to say that what we're doing could decide the outcome of the war.
Well, in that case, what are we standing around for? Let's get to work!
Hahaha, that's the spirit!
Andrew not only worked nonstop with no rest, but he also encouraged those working alongside him to work harder. In the end, Andrew and his workers succeeded in reconnecting the railroad in only four days.
Yahoo! We did it!

Andrew was given the task of managing the telegraph operators at the telegraph office. In the midst of a war, the telegraph office was constantly busy. Andrew was almost overwhelmed with the amount of telegrams he had to take care of.

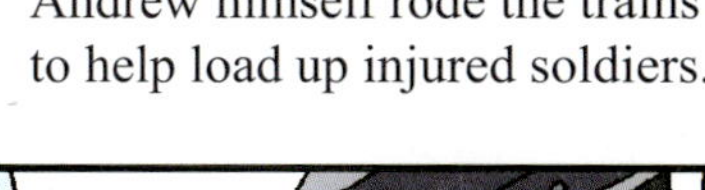

Andrew himself rode the trains to help load up injured soldiers.

Just hold on a little longer. It will be alright.

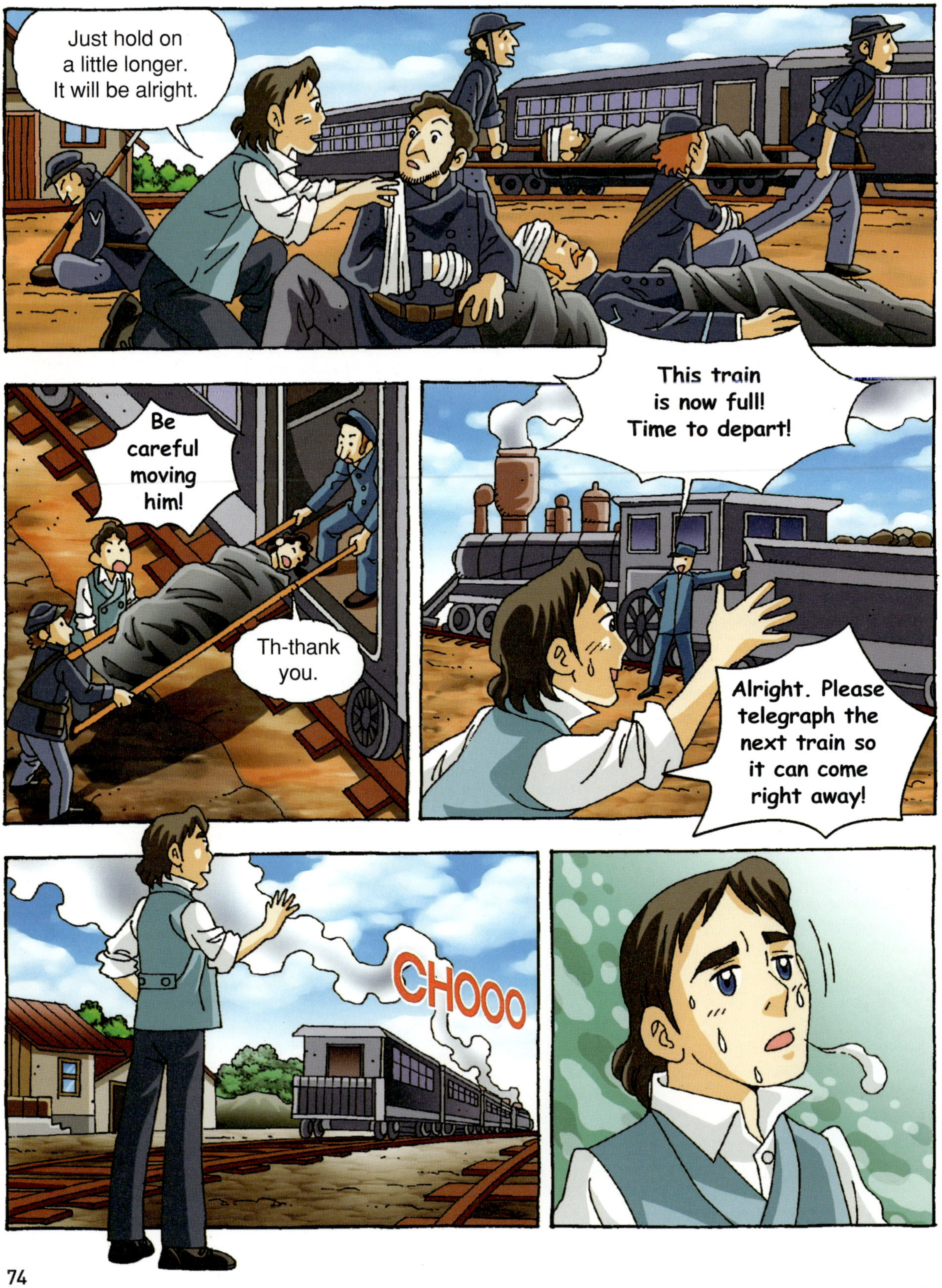

Be careful moving him!

Th-thank you.

This train is now full! Time to depart!

Alright. Please telegraph the next train so it can come right away!

CHOOO

The trains are playing a very big role in the warzone.

At that moment Andrew realized the real importance of the railroad: it would soon extend all across the land, and trains would provide the main means of transport for people and goods all over the country.

As the war was drawing to an end, Scott and Andrew moved to the command headquarters in Washington.
Any news?
Oh! Mr. President!
Haha, no need to act so surprised. Have you got any good news?
Yes, Sir. I'm pleased to inform you that the distribution of military supplies has been successfully completed.
I see. And what's your name?
Andrew Carnegie, sir.
Pleasure to meet you, Mr. Carnegie. I trust you will continue to be of assistance.
Assistance? I'm flattered, but I'm just a nobody, a telegraph operator...

No person is ever a "nobody." All people are equal. I am no different from you, Mr. Carnegie. As long as each person does the very best at the job they've been given, we can win the war.

President Lincoln's words made a deep impression on Andrew.

The President just said that we were equal.

Meanwhile, the Civil War had spurred unprecedented growth in the railroad. The Union army had begun constructing railroads in various places to transport soldiers across the country.

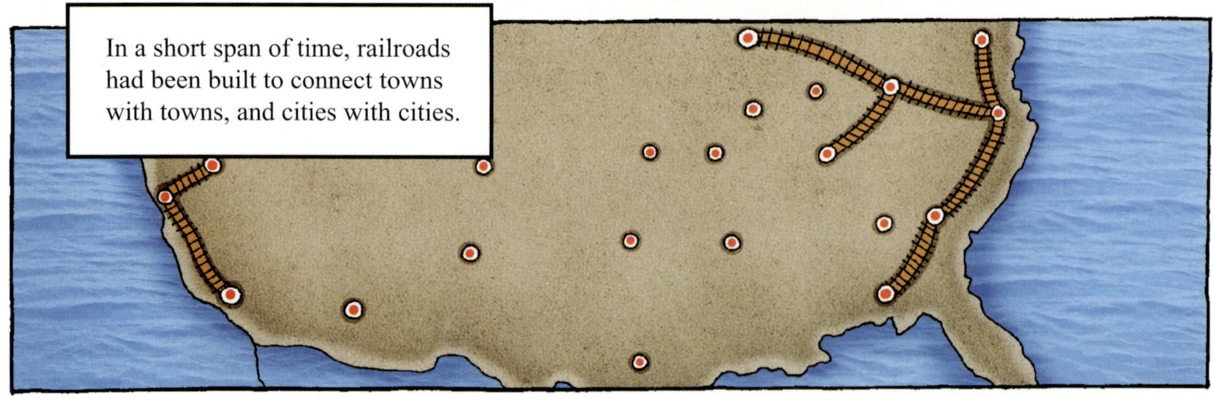
In a short span of time, railroads had been built to connect towns with towns, and cities with cities.

The era of the railroad had begun. Andrew started considering how he could best keep pace with all the new changes that were about to occur.
It's clear that we're about to enter the age of the railroad. But what can I do to be a part of it?
Well, the most important thing for the railroad industry is...
Already recognized as a talented telegraph operator, Andrew began dreaming of a new future for himself.
Iron?

05 The Birth of a Steel Magnate

The railroad industry developed very rapidly. Railroads were no longer limited to flat lands, for they now went through mountains and over rivers.

However, the bridges that trains had to cross were mostly made of wood, and thus not very safe.

Andrew thought it would be a good idea to make sturdier bridges for trains out of iron. So in 1863 he started a company called Keystone Bridge.

Andrew's decision to start an iron business was very wise. His company was flooded with new orders daily.
The Mississippi River? Yes, we can do that.
A bridge across the Ohio River? But of course.

This river is 500 feet wide.
Can you make a bridge to cross such a wide river?

The more people learned about how sturdy iron bridges were, the more popular Keystone Bridge became.

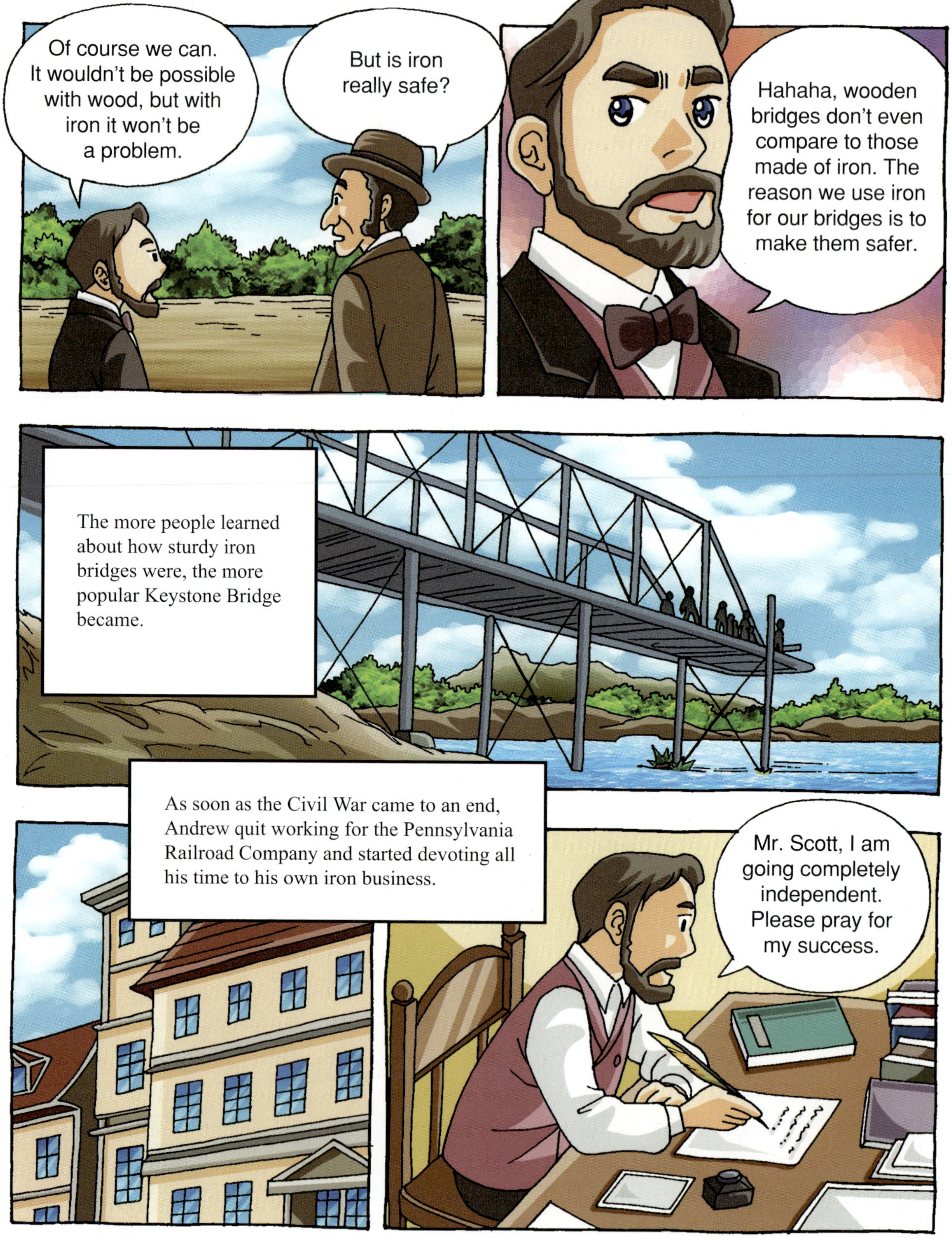

As soon as the Civil War came to an end, Andrew quit working for the Pennsylvania Railroad Company and started devoting all his time to his own iron business.

However, there was a problem with iron.

PSHHHHH

I can't believe it. The iron has melted again. We've got to change the tracks every few months because of this...

What's this? The iron is melting?

We're considering changing back to wooden tracks. Using iron is just too expensive.
This is the letter I received. Isn't there some way we can fix this problem?
Mr. Carnegie, isn't that just a characteristic of iron? It's only natural that it would have to be replaced every few months.
That's exactly why our maintenance costs are so high. If things continue as they are now, the iron industry won't have a bright future.

Our future depends on how we handle this.
Let's think about this for a bit. Anyone have an idea?
What if you make the tracks out of steel? It can be used for years without any problems.
But the cost of producing steel is too expensive.
Is there no way to make sturdy products from iron alone?
Mr. Carnegie, have you read the news about a man in England named Henry Bessemer? He's apparently succeeded in simplifying the process of making steel.

A simplified process?

Yes. He's discovered a completely new process that greatly cuts the cost of production.

But even in England Bessemer's process hasn't proven very popular. If his process is really what he claims it to be, that shouldn't be the case.

I've got to see this in person.

Andrew traveled to Europe to personally check out Bessemer's new technology.
KNOCK
KNOCK
Mr. Andrew Carnegie? The American steelworks businessman?
Follow me. There's a factory nearby.
That's correct. I've come to see your method of making steel.
Well, I'm honored.
You see that egg-shaped thing over there?
Yes. What's that?

Until now, steel was made by going through a number of difficult steps. But by using this revolving furnace, it can be done in one step.
Can you show me how it works?
Of course. It can produce steel in ten minutes.
Start the machine!
FOOOSH
SPLUTTER

*pig iron: Crude iron produced in a blast furnace and poured into moulds in preparation for making wrought iron, steels, alloys, etc.

So why hasn't this factory that you developed been accepted in England? Is there a problem?
No, no, that's not the case. Let's just say it's due to jealousy.
All the steel mills in England know of my technology, but they're afraid they will lose a lot of jobs if they use it.
Actually I don't know much about steel-making technology.
But what I do know is that your technique is definitely innovative.
Will you grant me permission to use your technology in my American steel mill?
Hahaha! Consider it done, Mr. Carnegie!

Back in the U.S, although Andrew had made up his mind to start producing steel, his investors were not so easily convinced.
Andrew, aren't you already very successful? Why start the difficult process of making steel now?
There are limits to current ironworks, because iron becomes unusable after just a few months. But this limitation can be overcome if we use steel instead.
But doesn't that mean you sell more iron if it all has to be replaced every few months? If everyone uses this sturdy steel you mentioned, people won't need to buy it as often...
Which means that your profits will be even less than they are now.
...

And that means that I, as an investor, will also lose money. Am I wrong?
Anyway, I'm against it.
I'm against it, too.
Think a bit farther ahead. If we continue to only produce inferior quality iron, the business will stop developing, and growth will come to a halt.
Not one to give up, Andrew sought out new investors. However, most of them just shook their heads in disagreement.

Andrew still didn't give up. Eventually he found an investor who thought as he did.
Alright, let's do this together.
Thank you, sir.
Now that he had collected sufficient investment capital, Andrew created the Edgar Thomson Steel Works, which began making steel around the clock.
Most of the people who had thought his idea ill-conceived started ridiculing him.
Hey, did you hear about Andrew?
I heard he found an investor and started making steel.
Haha, so he went ahead with his venture. I'm glad I steered clear of that one.
You're right. There's clearly no money to be made in steel.

Meanwhile, Andrew was out trying to spread the word about the steel his factory was making.
This is steel, you say?

Yes, when made of steel, these rails won't bend over time like iron rails do.

I can trust you, right?
Of course.

A few months later, the steel Andrew produced started to show its true value.
CHUGGA
CHUGGA

CHOO
CHOO

Carnegie's new steel was inexpensive and high quality, and it soon became very popular. Nonetheless, there were still some people who were suspicious of Carnegie's success.

The need for steel was steadily growing. Steel products had become popular, and everyone wanted to buy Carnegie's inexpensive, high-quality steel. In a short period of time, steel had spread all across America.

Mr. Carnegie, we have a problem!
We're out of iron.
What? How can we be running out of iron?
Orders are pouring in from all over the country, but we don't have enough raw iron to make the steel necessary to fill all the orders.
Oh my. We do have a problem.
With our current factory there's no way we can make enough steel to meet orders on time. The employees are getting exhausted, too.
Alright. I'll see what I can do.
Well well, and what brings Mr. Carnegie to our factory?

Would you happen to have any leftover scrap iron that you could sell? I'm low on materials to make steel.
What? You're joking, right? Do you really think one of your competitors is going to help you?
Andrew was surprised by how difficult it was to buy iron. Other companies were reluctant to sell him iron because they were jealous of his success. Andrew was very concerned.
That fact is that I simply can't buy any more iron right now.
Should I import iron from abroad? That will require a lot of time.
But I've made it this far, so it would be foolish to quit just because we're low on materials.
Mr. Carnegie, we've got a problem. The price of iron has skyrocketed.
What?

98

*iron ore mine: A mine from which iron ore, a base component of manufactured steel, can be extracted.

However, just when Andrew thought things were returning to normal, another problem emerged.
Everyone, stand clear! It's starting again!
What's happening?
It's no big deal. It's just inferior materials. It happens from time to time.
Inferior?
Yeah, it happens when there's less air inserted than normal. But don't worry. We discard everything that comes out defective.
You discard it?

After finding out that a large amount of inferior steel was coming out of his factory, Andrew wondered if there was a way to eliminate such failures altogether.

Why would you need a scientist like me for your steel making business?

I'd like to ask you to try to find a way to reduce the amount of inferior product we are producing. It would save me a lot of money.

Hm, if that's the case, then there must be a problem in the process of melting and solidifying the iron...

You've already pinpointed where the problem is! Professor, please help me to once again make inexpensive, good-quality steel.

Andrew hired scientists to refine his steel manufacturing process. Soon they succeeded in using technology to make the steel making process faster and error-free. Moreover, the price of production could be reduced even more, allowing Andrew to sell better steel at an even cheaper price.

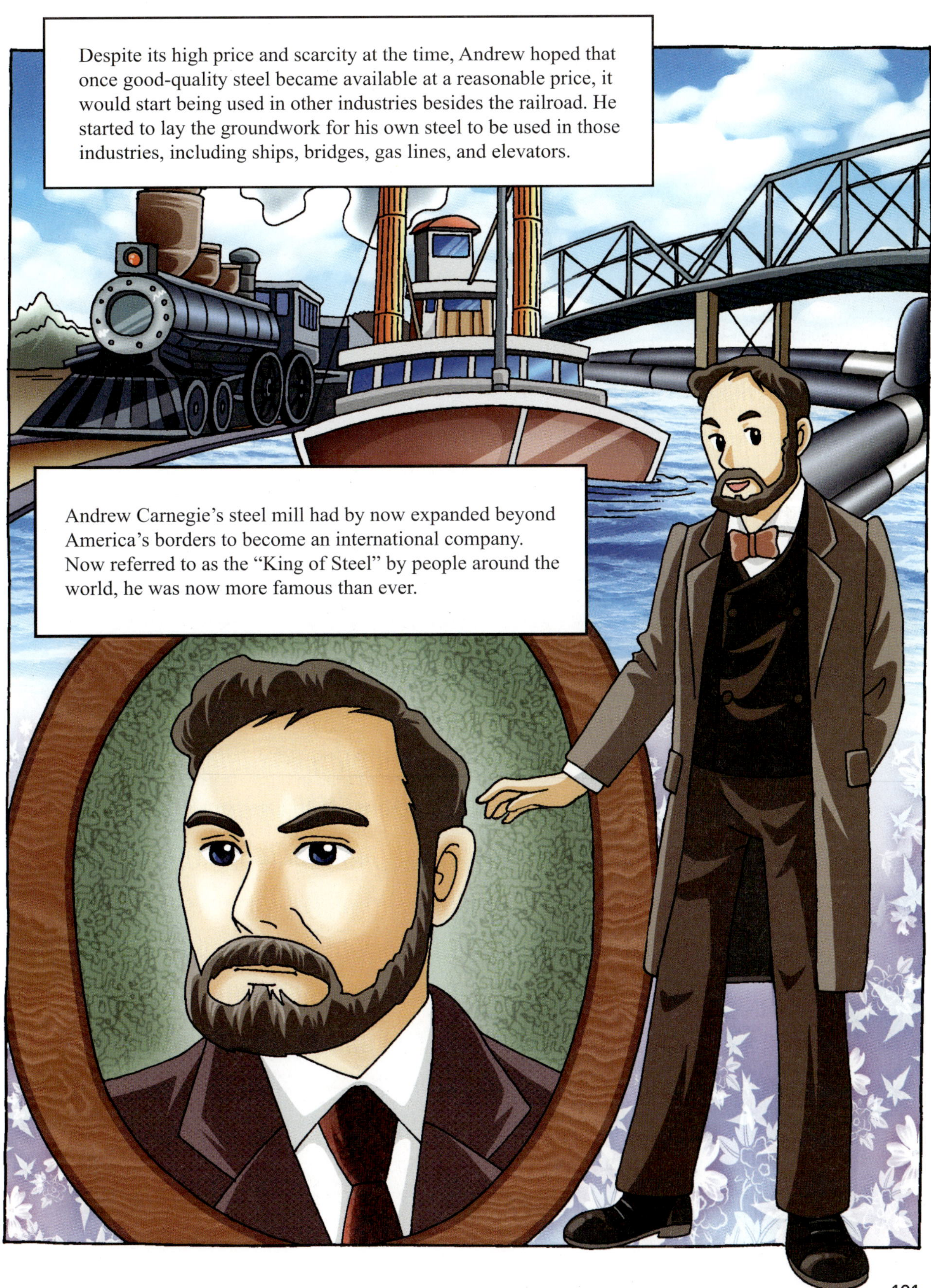

Despite its high price and scarcity at the time, Andrew hoped that once good-quality steel became available at a reasonable price, it would start being used in other industries besides the railroad. He started to lay the groundwork for his own steel to be used in those industries, including ships, bridges, gas lines, and elevators.

Andrew Carnegie's steel mill had by now expanded beyond America's borders to become an international company. Now referred to as the "King of Steel" by people around the world, he was now more famous than ever.

06 The Homestead Strike

Andrew had suddenly become the richest man in the world. As the head of his company, he was soon in charge of dozens of steel mills, thousands of employees, and hundreds of managers to oversee the employees.

As the company expanded, however, Andrew invested more time in business matters rather than taking care of his facilities and looking after his employees.

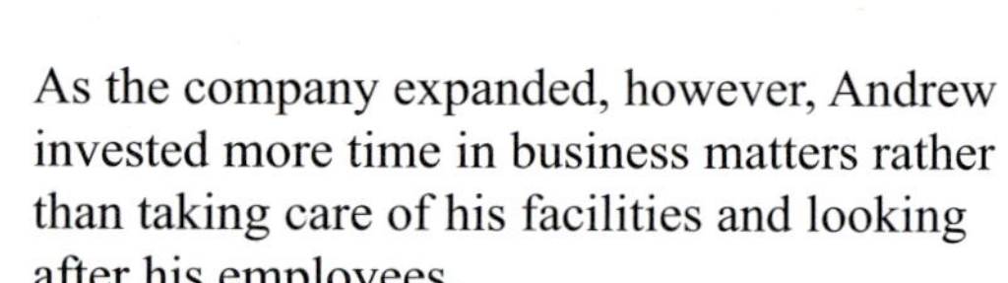

*labor union: A group organized by laborers for the purpose of serving the interests of all member laborers.

The dissatisfaction among employees grew day by day. Then one day, a strike* occurred at one of the Carnegie Steel Company's steel mills, the Homestead Steel Mill. At the time, Andrew was enjoying time with his family back in Scotland.

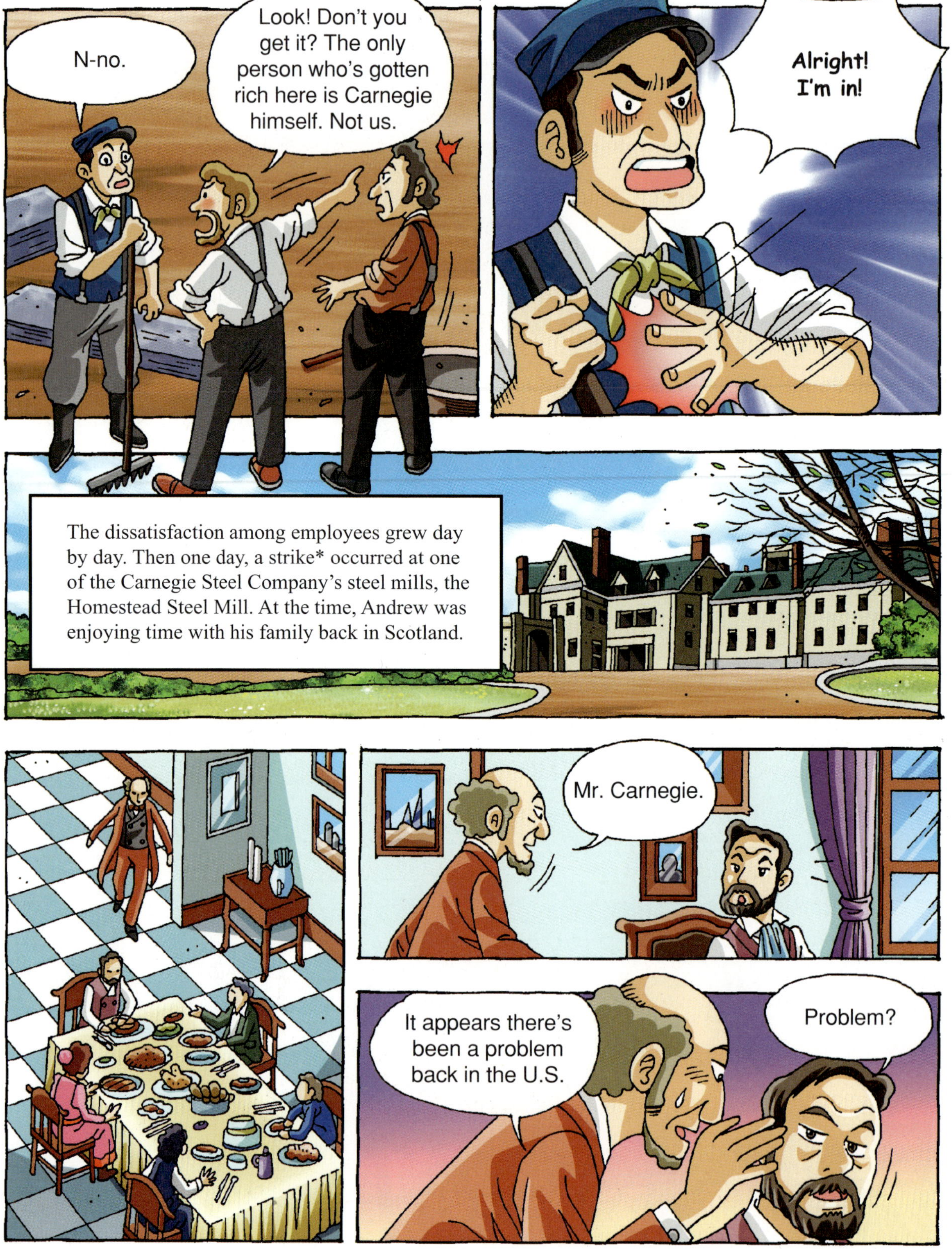

*strike: A temporary stoppage of work, done in protest.

The workers at the Homestead Steel Mill have gone on strike to demand higher wages.
Strike? This is bad, very bad. Who's in charge at that mill?
Mr. Frick.
Please continue to eat. I'll be back in a few minutes.
We can't survive like this!
We demand higher wages!

Contrary to what he had promised to Andrew, Frick made no effort to meet and talk with the workers. He simply tried to fix the problem as soon as possible.

As soon as night had fallen, Frick hired guards to block off the entrance to the mill.

Heard the news? The steel mill has closed off its entrance and hired armed guards.

If we don't do something we'll soon all be out on the streets without a job. We won't stand for this!

The angry workers tried to open the gates and enter the mill, but the attempt ended in a confrontation with the armed guards.

What did you say? This is our workplace!

Don't come any closer or we'll shoot!

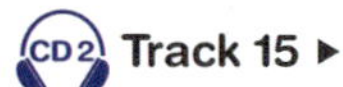

Meanwhile, Andrew, still in Scotland, received some very shocking news.

Mr. Carnegie, I think you're going to have to return to America.

Do you mean right now?

The strike at the Homestead Mill...

If that's what this is about, I've already instructed Frick to take care of it.

Yes, but it seems that he wasn't able to deal with it successfully. The guards that Frick hired had a confrontation with the workers, and some deaths have been reported.

D-deaths? People have died? At my factory?
Y-yes, sir. That's why I think you should go there personally, Mr. Carnegie.

Was there some problem at my company that would cause the workers to risk their lives fighting?

Ah, I haven't been treating my workers like they deserve to be treated. This isn't Frick's fault. It's mine.

American newspapers reported on the Homestead Strike, and they were critical of Andrew.
Is Carnegie's Wealth All for Himself?
Worker and Guard Skirmish Results in Dozens of Casualties!
Carnegie Continues Vacation amid Mayhem
Where in the World Is Irresponsible Carnegie?

Mr. Carnegie! How did all this happen?

I still don't know enough about what happened. I'll talk to all of you later.
Were you unaware of what was happening?
What did you do in Scotland?
The Homestead Mill Complex, which was always bustling with activity, had become a ghost town.

If it had been me, I wouldn't have done what you did.

Frick.

Mr. Czarnegie, if we raise the workers' wages, then we'll have to raise the prices of our products, too. Then we would no longer be known as the company of inexpensive, high-quality goods.

Frick, do you consider that more important than the lives our employees?

No, I don't, but...

We're going to shut this mill down until we get this straightened out. I need you to call a carriage.
Carriage? Why...
Don't you think I ought to visit the families of the dead workers to offer our apologies?
No, you can't do that! The other workers will surely attack you.
Get the carriage ready! Now!
Carnegie set off for the area where the Homestead Steel Mill workers lived.

I don't believe it, it's Carnegie himself! What on earth did he come here for?
And just what brings the distinguished Mr. Carnegie to these lowly parts?

I sincerely apologize. I take full responsibility for everything.
He's clearly got something up his sleeve! Don't be fooled!
We don't buy it!

I deeply regret the way this situation has turned out.

We won't fall for any of your tricks! You'd better turn around and leave now if you don't want to get hurt!
Out of our way!
We don't need your apology!
I'll keep apologizing until all of your anger dies down. And, I want to let everyone know just how strongly I care about this.
Care? You want to show your "care" for us by throwing us out into the streets?
No, not at all. Everyone, in my mind, this company, its management, and its workers are like a three-legged chair.
What?

If the company is the chair, then it's supported by the three legs which are me, the management, you, the workers, and capital.
And if even one of the three legs is removed, then the chair falls to the ground. This company is no different. Without all of you, our company would fall to the ground, helpless.

Although, Andrew did not accept all of the workers' demands, he carefully explained the company's side of the situation, and he made efforts to understand the workers' point of view.
While I cannot agree to all of your demands, I will do my best to make sure everyone has a better working environment.

Back at his company, Carnegie worked day and night to keep his promise to his workers.
Mr. Carnegie, you have a guest.
And you are...?
Mr. Carnegie, I'm the wife of one of the workers who died during the Homestead Strike.
Oh, really? Please come this way.
I see.
I don't know if I should be asking this, but I need your help. Since my husband died, here's no longer anyone in our family who can support us.

Look, Mr. Carnegie doesn't have time to listen to your story.
I know, but my son is hungry, and it's impossible for us to get by on the money I earn alone.
Do you think this is some kind of charity organization? Please leave now!
Wait!
Miss, don't you have any money saved?
It was hard for us to get by even with my husband's paychecks. I doubt you have an appreciation for that, Mr. Carnegie.

In that case, I'll help you out.
No, Mr. Carnegie. If you help this woman now, then countless others will come asking for the same.

I'll deal with what happens later.
Th-thank you, sir. Thank you so much.

After helping the woman, Carnegie took some time to reflect on what had happened.

Actually, I lend out my books every Saturday.
All people are equal.
You don't think firing the employees is a bit harsh?
I received the help of numerous people to get where I am today. Why did it take me so long to realize this?
My wealth does not belong just to me. All of this was created together with my employees, no, with people everywhere.
Now it's time to give it all back.

07 A Glorious Retirement

Andrew set up an organization for his philanthropic projects and began the task of distributing his wealth back to society. Letters asking for Carnegie's help started pouring in from all across America.

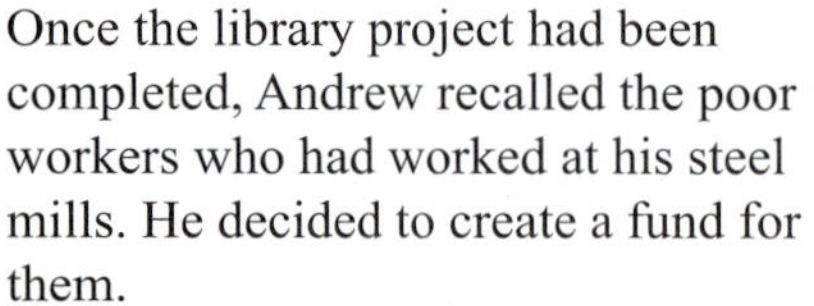

Once the library project had been completed, Andrew recalled the poor workers who had worked at his steel mills. He decided to create a fund for them.

Hey, look at this!

What is it?
Mr. Carnegie created the "Andrew Carnegie Relief Fund." He made it specifically for us workers whose efforts haven't been properly acknowledged! Now even those of us who have already retired can also receive assistance.
Is-is that true?

Yes, it says it will provide for those retired with no income and those needing help in old age. Let's sign up immediately!
I can think of no better blessing than this...

124

Mr. Carnegie, you have a guest.
Who is it?

It's the principal of a high school asking for a donation.
Please let him in.

CREAK

Puff!

He's blowing out candles in the dark. His promise to give away all of his wealth must have been a lie. Surely a man so stingy about a single candle wouldn't really give away all his money?
Please have a seat. May I ask what brings you here?
Our school is in the process of fixing up its facilities so that we can provide a better environment for our students. I was wondering if it might be possible to get your assistance with some of the costs.
What you're doing is a very good thing. The education of our children is very important. I will happily help you out.
What?
Why are you surprised?

Mr. Carnegie, I had no idea it would be so easy to ask you for assistance. I thought I would really have to beg and plead for my cause.
Why would you think that?
When I first walked in, you blew out a candle. I thought that a man so stingy about one candle would not easily part with a large amount of money.
I see there's been a misunderstanding. I need two candles when reading, but only one, when having a conversation with someone. That's why I extinguished one of them.
Wow, even with so much wealth he still takes care not to waste a candle!

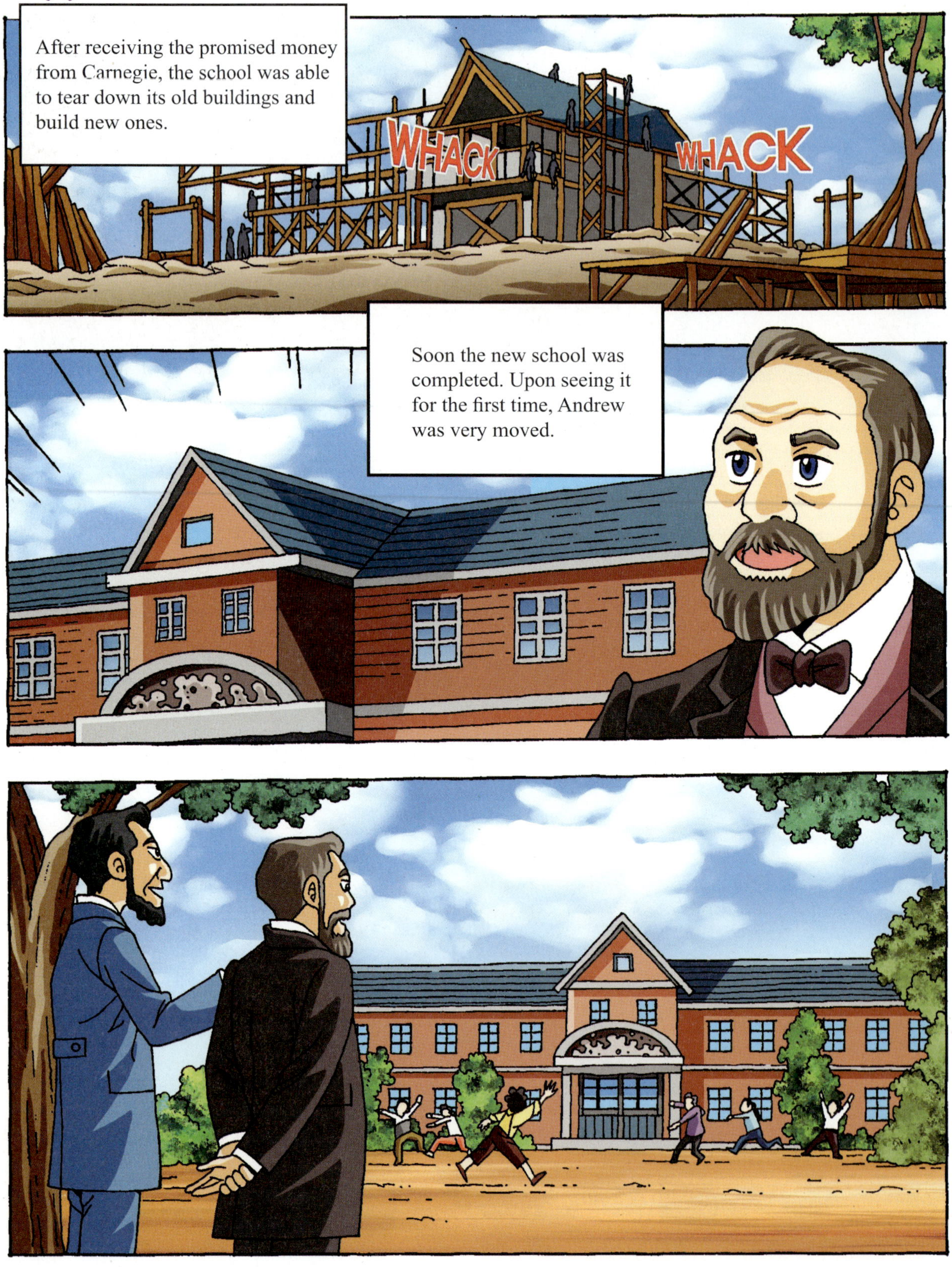

After receiving the promised money from Carnegie, the school was able to tear down its old buildings and build new ones.

Soon the new school was completed. Upon seeing it for the first time, Andrew was very moved.

Sir, I must tell you how great it makes me feel to see all the kids playing so happily.
Haha, and the kids are very thankful. Mr. Carnegie, for making their school a better place. Why don't we take this opportunity to say hello to them.

No, that's okay. You don't need to do that.

Andrew felt an indescribable happiness. Compared to his past business pursuits, the joy of giving to others was like nothing he had ever felt before.

Andrew realized the importance of education after seeing how happy the school kids had been. The proper cultivation of every child's dreams for the future was of utmost importance in the field of education. Andrew thus decided to establish the "Carnegie Foundation for the Advancement of Teaching" to help fund science and educational enterprises.

The Carnegie Foundation established astronomy observatories and universities that greatly assisted knowledge industries.

Not long ago, this spot was barren land. But now there's a wonderful university here. I feel like I've become Aladdin, and just by rubbing my magic lamp this university has appeared.

Pittsburgh is where my company started, and nothing would please me more than to be able give something back to the city. It is my hope that Carnegie Technical Schools will turn out many great talented individuals.

The university Andrew created was later merged with Mellon Institute of Industrial Research to create Carnegie Mellon University. The university grew to become one of America's leading computer science and engineering universities.
CLAP
CLAP
YAY
CLAP

The extent of Andrew's philanthropic efforts was unprecedented. An individual person had never before given way so much money. His methods of distributing his donations systematically through his foundations attracted much attention.

I later became interested in culture and art that could be appreciated by our increasingly educated society. So I started building theaters and performance venues that could be enjoyed by everyone.
But of all those endeavors, there must be one that you deem most important...
No, there is not. I consider every dollar I donate to be equally important. If my money can be used for a good cause, then I will gladly support that cause. However!
Excuse me?
I am staunchly opposed to my money being used, in any form or fashion, for unjust purposes. War is a perfect example.

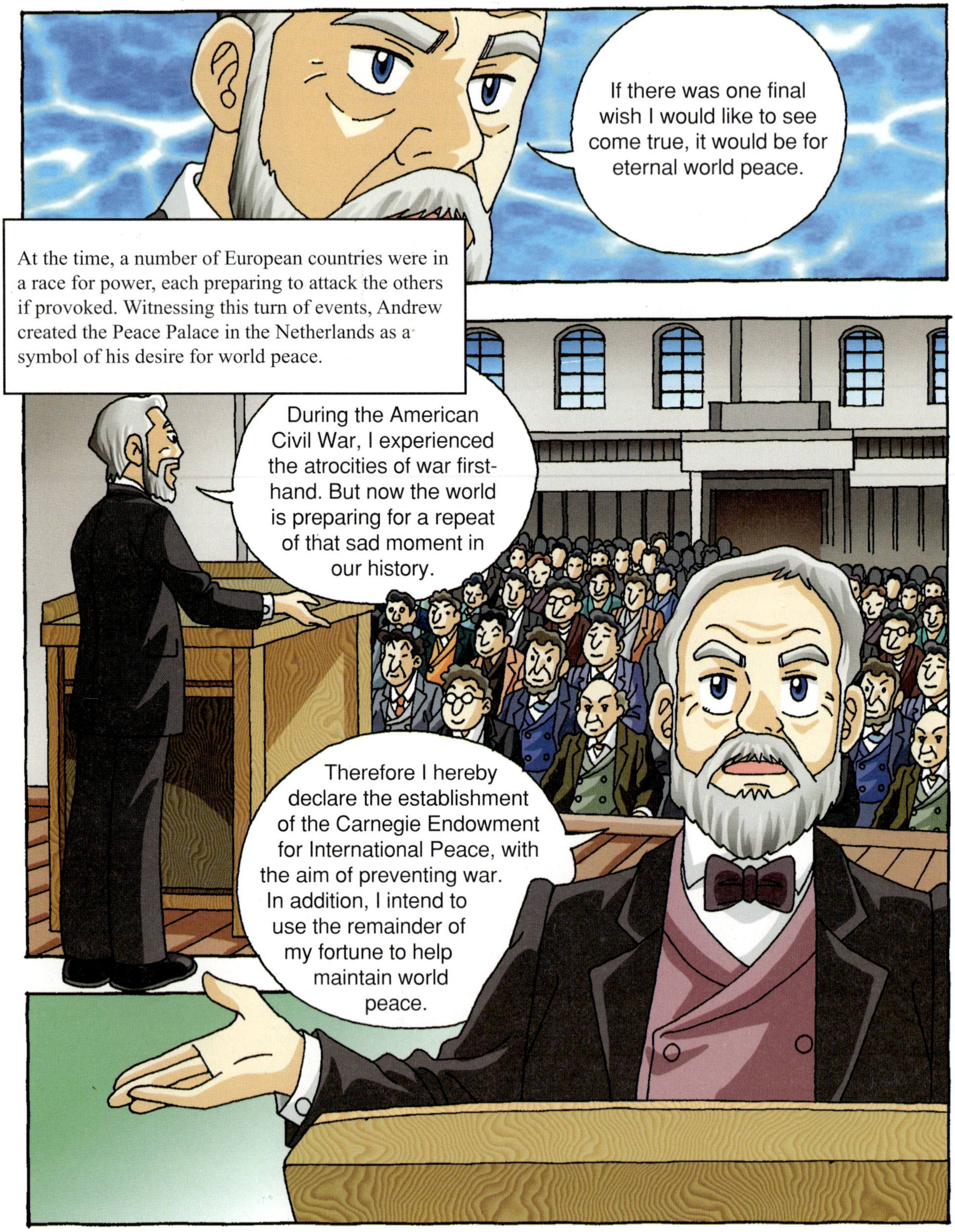

At the time, a number of European countries were in a race for power, each preparing to attack the others if provoked. Witnessing this turn of events, Andrew created the Peace Palace in the Netherlands as a symbol of his desire for world peace.

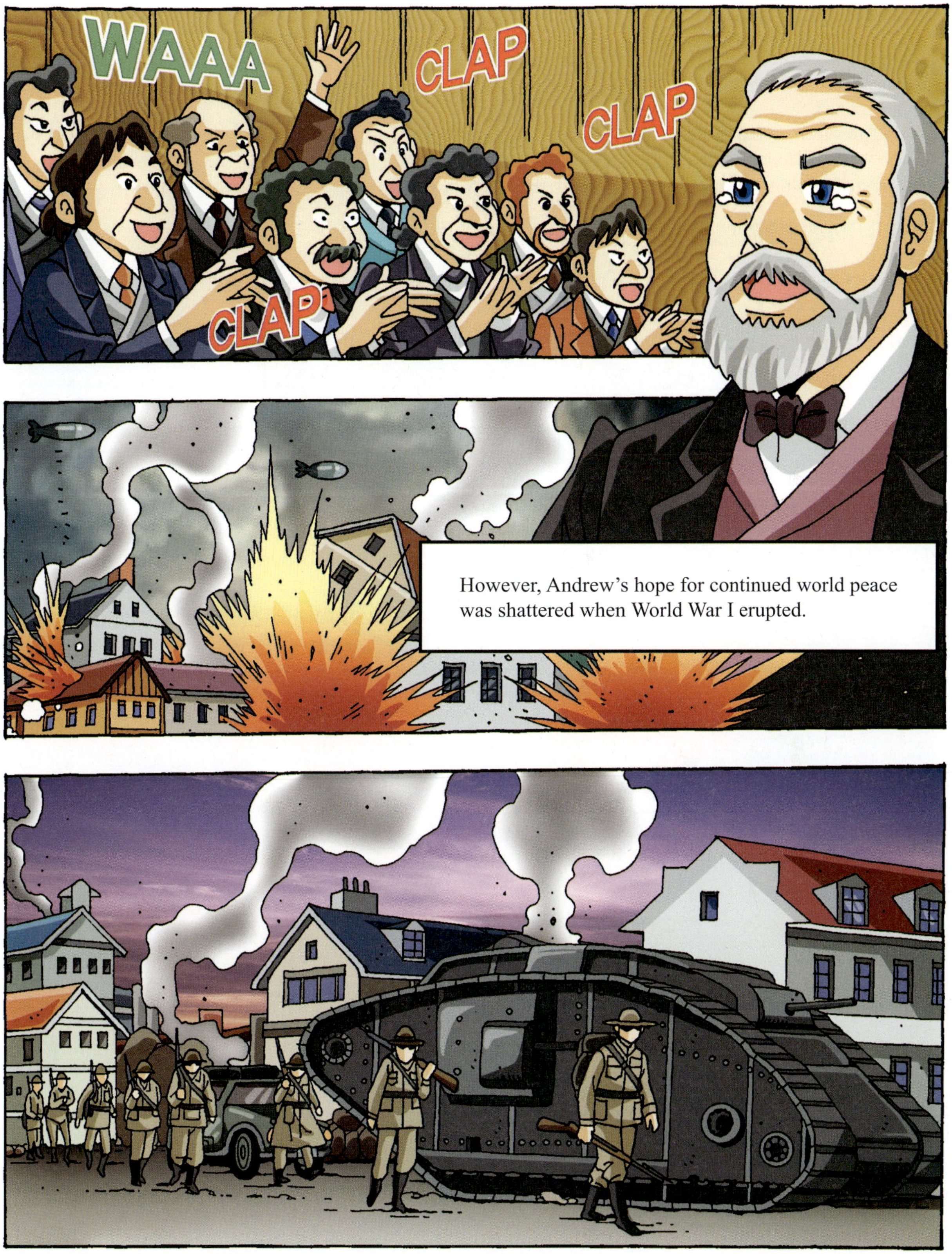

However, Andrew's hope for continued world peace was shattered when World War I erupted.

Andrew became very worried upon hearing that the war had begun. He fell sick, and each piece of tragic news about the war only made his condition worse.

His condition developed into pneumonia, which took his life on August 11, 1919. Although the war eventually ended, Andrew Carnegie never woke up.

Although Andrew Carnegie was very successful as a steel magnate, he is admired even more as a great philanthropist. In total, he constructed more than 3,000 libraries.

He also donated more than 8,000 pipe organs to institutions all around the world, so that people everywhere could enjoy their beautiful sounds, and he created theaters where anyone could go and enjoy a performance.

By creating a relief fund for workers and a railroad fund for his previous employer, the railroad, Andrew was able to help countless individuals have a better life after retirement.

He built universities so students could study to their hearts content, including universities for alienated black students. Finally, he built numerous astronomical observatories to enable us to see even more of the universe.

From the time he announced his retirement at age 67 until his death, he gave his 480 million dollar fortune back to society. In today's dollars, that amount would be the equivalent of almost 50 billion dollars.

Andrew Carnegie once said the following: "I have had two lives. One was a life of making money, and the other was a life of giving it. I found that a life of giving made me infinitely happier."

Although Andrew Carnegie spent the majority of his life as a businessman, he is more widely known for his later work as a philanthropist. He generously donated money to wherever it was necessary, regardless of the location or type of institution. As a result, the entire world benefited from Carnegie's generous donations. Even today, the Carnegie Foundation actively helps those in need around the world, in the same spirit as Andrew himself would have done. Today we can meet the great philanthropist Andrew Carnegie by visiting any one of the many buildings that bear his name.

Word Search

● Find the words which are hidden horizontally, vertically and diagonally.

```
W A F F O R D G Q M Z G Q Q M Z G Q M X
W O I N A E N T I O N H W W N A H C T O
E B M J A B Q J E E T A R B A R I O U M
R T C P R D C K R X V K R R V C K I D M
E C H O A S E S U P P L I E S D U M E E
V X E R Y N E O Y E N Q Y Y X E N W C M
E Z V W E D I W C R X W R U Z V J N O W
A N A E I A E O A I E C E I A R A E D I
L S I R O S D C N E L R H O S C S R E T
P D C U P D H T O N I E O P D O T B D P
L F R Y H F U Y A C C Y V A F N Y I F L
K G S U S T I N C E A G E I N F U T G A
T H D I D H M I D H L I R D H I I Y H L
O J G B S O R A F J T J F F J D J F J H
A C C O M P L I S H I O N A T E B G K I
H L O N H L E N H E E N H H L N N H L B
J Q D M J Q T A U T D O R I T C M J B L
L W E Q L W Y Q L W Y Q L L W E Q L U E
Z W R E B W N T Z W K F Z Z S U F T J R
X E M E X M R I N C P Y S T U R E X N M
W R Q C C R Q U A L I T Y T R Q M C R P
```

afford	experience	accomplish	supplies
decode	quality	thread	confidence

Vocabulary

● Match each word to the correct meaning.

1. weaver
2. Industrial Revolution
3. opportunity
4. shabby
5. paycheck
6. telegraph messenger
7. telegram
8. ambition
9. railroad
10. Civil War
11. communicate
12. apologize

• 월급
• 직조공
• 산업 혁명
• 기회
• 낡은, 허름한
• 철도
• 남북 전쟁
• 전신 전달원
• 전보
• 야망
• 사과하다
• 의사소통하다

Guess What?

● Guess what he said in the blank.

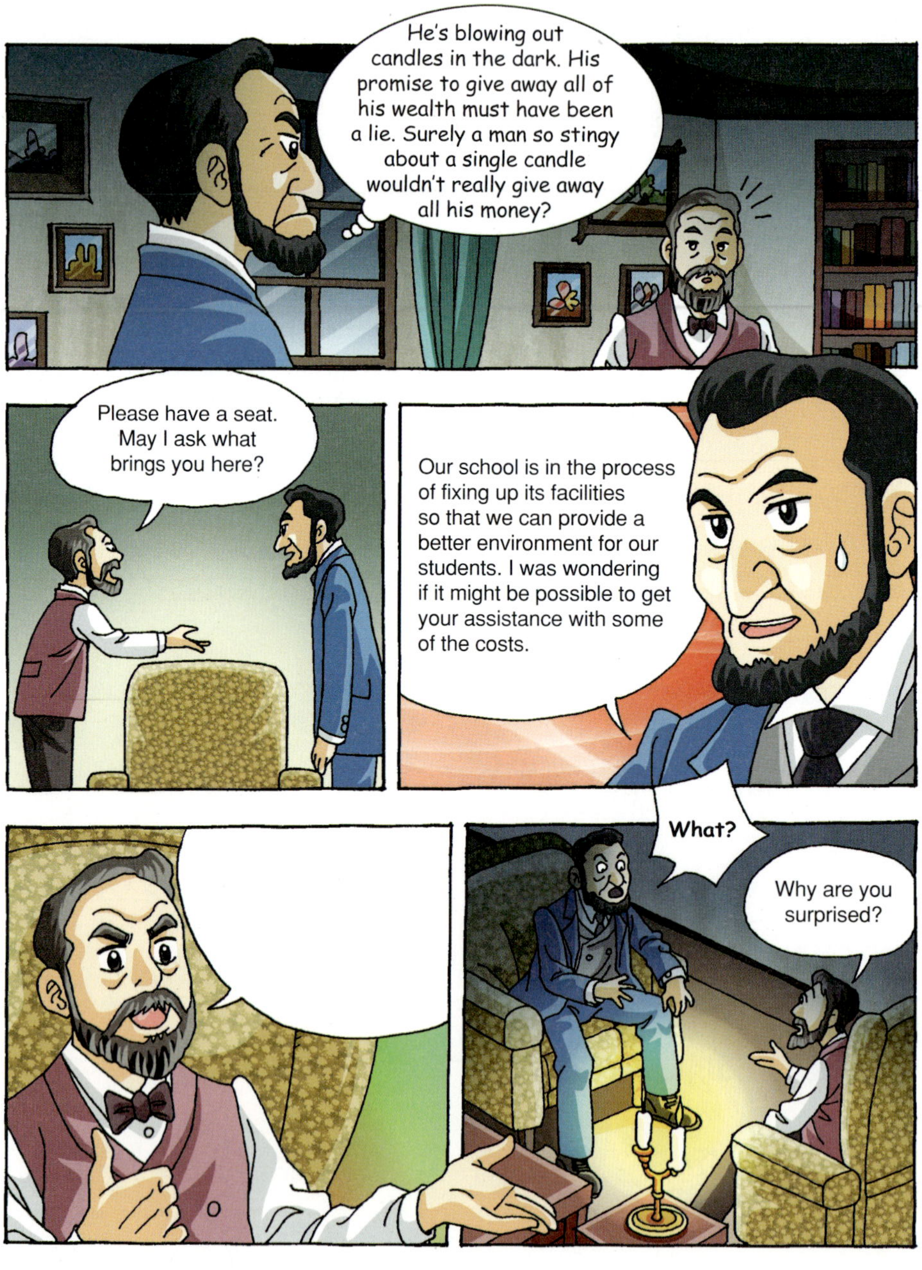

4 If I Were a Billionaire

Andrew Carnegie(1835~1919) was probably the first to state publicly that the rich should have a moral obligation to give away their fortunes for the benefit of the world. During his life time, he gave away over 350 million dollars. For example, he built 2,509 public libraries with over 56 million dollars.

▲ If you were a billionaire like Andrew Carnegie, what would you do in order to make the world better? Make a list of your activities to improve the society.

5 Transportation

● Let's check out the history of transportation.

3500 BC	The first wheel was invented by the Sumarians, the first civilization. Wheeled carts and chariots were used. River boats with oars were invented.
2000 BC	Horses were domesticated and used for transportation.
800 BC	Horseshoes were used.
181	The wheelbarrow is invented in China.
1492	Leonardo da Vinci wrote and sketched ideas for flying machines.
1620	Cornelius Van Drebbel made the first submarine of 3~4 m in length that could stay under water for a couple of hours.
1662	Blaise Pascal designed the first horse-drawn public bus that ran on a regular route and schedule, and had a fare system.
1740	Jacques de Vaucanson invented the first clockwork powered carriage.
1769	Nicolas Joseph Cugnot invented and used the first self-powered road vehicle using a steam engine. He also crashed it into a wall and became the first recorded road vehicle accident.
1783	The French brothers Joseph Montgolfier and Etienne Montgolfier invented the first hot air balloons.
1783	Marquis Claude Francoirs de Jouffroy d'Abbans used steam with a paddle wheel to power a steamboat.
1787	John Fitch made the first successful steamboat trail on the Delaware Rivers.
1790	Modern bicycles were invented and began being used.
1801	Richard Trevithick invented the first steam powered locomotive designed for roads.

제임스 와트의 증기 기관 ⓒNicolas Perez

증기 기관으로 동력을 얻는 증기 기관차 ⓒAshley Dace

1807	Isaac de Rivas made the first hydrogen gas powered vehicle. The first steamboat with regular passenger service.
1814	The first practical steam-powered engine was built by George Stephenson.
1858	Jean Lenoir invented the first gasoline powered automobile.
1867	The first gas-powered bicycle was invented.
1871	The first cable car was invented by Andrew Smith Hallidie.
1885	Karl Benz built the first practical automobile with an internal-combustion engine for actual use.
1899	Ferdinand von Zeppelin built the first successful air blimp.
1903	The Wright Brothers invented and flew the first engined airplane.
1908	Henry Ford made an improved assembly line for automobile manufacturing.
1911	Selandia launched the first ship to sail the ocean run by diesel engines.
1926	The first liquid-fueled rockets were built and launched.
1940	The first successful helicopter was built.
1947	The first supersonic jets were flown.
1956	Hovercraft was invented.
1964	The first bullet train was invented.
1969	The first manned mission to the moon was launched. Neil Armstrong became the first man to set foot on the moon.
1976	Concorde became the world's first commercial passenger supersonic aircraft.
1981	Space shuttle was launched by NASA.

1835년		11월 25일, 스코틀랜드 던펌린에서 태어났습니다.
1848년	13세	가족과 함께 미국으로 이민을 갑니다. 방적 공장에서 보빈 보이로 일하게 됩니다.
1850년	15세	전보 배달원을 거쳐 전신 기사로 일합니다.
1853년	18세	펜실베니아 철도 회사로 옮깁니다.
1859년	24세	펜실베니아 철도 피츠버그 지국의 책임자가 됩니다.
1861년	26세	남북 전쟁이 시작되어 워싱턴에서 일합니다.
1863년	28세	키스톤 브리지라는 철 회사를 설립합니다.
1872년	37세	영국의 헨리 베세머를 만나 강철을 생산하기로 결심합니다.
1875년	40세	자신이 세운 에드거 톰슨 제강소에서 본격적인 강철 생산을 시작합니다.
1887년	52세	루이즈 화이트필드와 결혼합니다.

1889년 54세 에세이 『부의 복음』을 출간합니다.
　　　　　　　이 책에서 부자의 사회적 책임에 대해 언급합니다.

1892년 57세 홈스테드 제강소에서 노동자들의 파업이 발생하여 인명 피해가 납니다.

1897년 62세 딸 마거릿이 태어납니다.

1899년 64세 카네기가 가진 제강소들을 모두 합쳐 '카네기 제강소'가 탄생하였습니다.

1900년 65세 경영에서 은퇴하고 본격적으로 자선 사업만을 하기로 결심합니다.

1902년 67세 카네기 협회를 설립했습니다.

1905년 70세 카네기 교육 진흥 재단을 설립했습니다.

1907년 72세 피츠버그 대학을 설립합니다.

1910년 75세 세계 평화를 위한 카네기 국제 평화 재단을 설립했습니다.

1914년 79세 1차 세계 대전이 발발합니다. 평화를 기원했던 카네기는 크게 실망합니다.

1919년 84세 8월 11일, 폐렴이 악화되어 사망합니다.

who? 01	Barack Obama	978-89-6370-514-9
who? 02	Charles Darwin	978-89-6370-515-6
who? 03	Bill Gates	978-89-6370-516-3
who? 04	Hillary Clinton	978-89-6370-517-0
who? 05	Stephen Hawking	978-89-6370-518-7
who? 06	Oprah Winfrey	978-89-6370-519-4
who? 07	Steven Spielberg	978-89-6370-520-0
who? 08	Thomas Edison	978-89-6370-521-7
who? 09	Abraham Lincoln	978-89-6370-522-4
who? 10	Martin Luther King, Jr.	978-89-6370-523-1
who? 11	Louis Braille	978-89-6370-439-5
who? 12	Albert Einstein	978-89-6370-440-1
who? 13	Jane Goodall	978-89-6370-441-8
who? 14	Walt Disney	978-89-6370-442-5
who? 15	Winston Churchill	978-89-6370-443-2
who? 16	Warren Buffett	978-89-6370-444-9
who? 17	Nelson Mandela	978-89-6370-445-6
who? 18	Steve Jobs	978-89-6370-446-3
who? 19	J. K. Rowling	978-89-6370-447-0
who? 20	Jean-Henri Fabre	978-89-6370-448-7
who? 21	Vincent van Gogh	978-89-6370-449-4
who? 22	Marie Curie	978-89-6370-450-0
who? 23	Henry David Thoreau	978-89-6370-451-7
who? 24	Andrew Carnegie	978-89-6370-452-4
who? 25	Coco Chanel	978-89-6370-453-1
who? 26	Charlie Chaplin	978-89-6370-454-8
who? 27	Ho Chi Minh	978-89-6370-455-5
who? 28	Ludwig van Beethoven	978-89-6370-456-2
who? 29	Mao Zedong	978-89-6370-457-9
who? 30	Kim Dae-jung	978-89-6370-458-6